CONDORS IN
CANYON COUNTRY

SOPHIE A. H. OSBORN

CONDORS IN CANYON COUNTRY

THE RETURN OF THE CALIFORNIA CONDOR TO THE GRAND CANYON REGION

GRAND CANYON ASSOCIATION

Grand Canyon Association
P.O. Box 399
Grand Canyon, AZ 86023-0399
(800) 858-2808
www.grandcanyon.org

Printed in China on recycled paper using soy-based inks
Edited by Todd R. Berger
Maps by Rick Wheeler
Designed by Campana Design | Nancy Campana

First Edition
11   10   09   08   07   1   2   3   4   5

Library of Congress Cataloging-in-Publication Data

Osborn, Sophie A. H.
  Condors in canyon country : the return of the California condor to
the Grand Canyon region / Sophie A. H. Osborn. — 1st ed.
        p. cm.
  Includes bibliographical references and index.
  ISBN-13: 978-0-938216-87-2; 978-0-938216-98-8 (pbk.)
  1. California condor. 2. California condor—Reintroduction—
Arizona—Grand Canyon Region. I. Title.
  QL696.C53O83 2007
  598.9'2—dc22
                        2006022934

*It is the mission of the Grand Canyon Association to cultivate knowledge,
discovery, and stewardship for the benefit of Grand Canyon National Park
and its visitors. Proceeds from the sale of this book will be used to support
the educational goals of Grand Canyon National Park.*

Pages ii–iii: A young, reintroduced California condor perched above the
Colorado River at Horseshoe Bend in the northeastern section of Grand
Canyon National Park. Condors were first reintroduced to the region in 1996.

Page v: Condor 392, a wild-hatched juvenile, was the third chick to be raised
successfully at Grand Canyon National Park.

Do not go gentle into that good night. . . .

Rage, rage against the dying of the light.

DYLAN THOMAS

DEDICATION

This book is dedicated to the memory of Condor 176, who disappeared forever in February 2004. To me, she was the wildest and most spectacular of all Arizona's condors.

To the unsung heroes, the dedicated field biologists, who have labored tirelessly day in and day out over months and years to keep the condors flying.

And most of all, to Chad, who has shared every moment of my time with condors, and who has been an equally passionate advocate for their success.

CONTENTS

ACKNOWLEDGMENTS

First and foremost, I thank the Grand Canyon Association for conceiving this book and for asking me to write it. I am grateful to them for giving me the opportunity to make a book on Arizona's condors a reality.

I thank my editor, Todd Berger, for his patience, encouragement, support, and skillful editing. This book was vastly improved through his efforts.

I thank Mike Wallace for generously sharing his extraordinary knowledge of condors (Andean and California), for always listening to and valuing my ideas regarding condor behavior and management, and for reviewing this manuscript. Mike arguably has contributed more than anyone else to the return of the California condor over the last twenty-five years. His expertise, academic contribution, field abilities, and passion for the condors are unparalleled.

I thank the staff at the Los Angeles Zoo, particularly Mike Clark, Chandra David, Debbie Sears, and Marti Jenkins, for countless informative discussions, for their passion for and dedication to raising the best possible condors for release, for showing me the behind-the-scenes details of captive breeding, and for letting me see a day-old condor chick—a sight I will always treasure. Special thanks to Mike Clark for generously sharing his extraordinary knowledge of condor behavior.

Thanks to Jan Hamber, who has given to condors for more than thirty years. To me she is the AC-8 of the condor world, and she will know that there is no higher praise. Thanks to Jan also for her stories, for her kindness and support, and for supplying me with difficult-to-access research material.

I thank Allan Mee for countless inspiring and motivating discussions about condors. Our times in Salt Creek and elsewhere were always a delight. Allan's contributions to our knowledge of condor breeding behavior have been extraordinary, and his persistence in fighting for the condors in the face of the disheartening episodes of trash ingestion by chicks in California is commendable.

Thank you to Shawn Farry for introducing me to condors, for enlightening me on condor behavior and management, and for inspiring me to follow in his impressive footsteps as the Peregrine Fund's condor Field Manager.

I thank the Condor Field Management Working Group, a gathering of field and zoo personnel, for enlightening discussions and for an unstinting commitment to condors. As the ones who worked with condors on a daily basis, we met to exchange our knowledge of field and rearing techniques and other condor issues. We left each meeting more impassioned, committed, and enlightened with regard to condor behavior and management.

I thank the many biologists who worked as field crew with me on the reintroduction project for their tireless efforts, staunch support, and strong friendships. Their efforts have kept condors flying in Arizona. Kris Lightner, Jill Adams, Kevin Fairhurst, Jonna Wiedmaier, Eddie Feltes, Chris Crowe, Blake Massey, Courtney Harris, Dave McGraw, Ty Donnely, Brandon Breen, Kate Parmentier, and Marta Curti in particular went above and beyond what was asked of them and, somehow, despite my endlessly exacting demands, became dear friends. They garnered my admiration, respect, loyalty, and gratitude.

I thank the staff of the Division of Interpretation at Grand Canyon National Park for tirelessly sharing their love and knowledge of condors with an ever-growing horde of fascinated park visitors. I am particularly grateful to Pam Cox, Marker Marshall, Pat and Ron Brown, and Allyson Mathis for their dedication to and enthusiasm about condors. Special thanks to Marker and Pam for their careful review of the manuscript.

I thank Joe Burnett and Kelly Sorenson of the Ventana Wilderness Society for many fruitful discussions, for enlightening trips to their Central California Release Site at Big Sur, for their unwavering support of my efforts, and for trying to provide me with opportunities to stay involved with condors.

I thank the many people who wrote to me in support of the "Notes from the Field" I wrote for the Peregrine Fund's Web site. Their kind words, encouragement, and thanks gave me inspiration and confidence to continue writing about condors, and provided me with e-mail friends from California to Scotland.

I thank Jim Mead of the University of Arizona for educating me about Pleistocene issues, for stimulating discussions, and most of all for showing me condor bones dating from the Pleistocene Age and a magnificent 12,000-year-old condor skull.

I thank Ron Jurek of the California Department of Fish and Game for helping me keep condor numbers straight throughout the years and for being so quick to respond to my barrage of e-mail questions.

I thank Lloyd Kiff for his quiet support, for his gift of the *Annals of Gymnogyps* (which I treasure), and for helping me with ideas for the Cost of the Condor Program sidebar in Chapter 7.

I thank Mike Mace of the San Diego Zoological Society for his efforts as keeper of the California Condor Studbook, which provided me with a wealth of information about individual condors and their relationships to one another.

I thank Kathy Sullivan of the Arizona Game and Fish Department for providing me with the latest updates on Arizona hunter purchases of nonlead ammunition and other valuable hunter-related numbers.

I thank Chris Parish, Project Director of the Peregrine Fund's condor reintroduction program, for his efforts on behalf of condors and for the good times we shared while doing what we believed was best for the Arizona birds.

A special thanks to my family, Mum, Lisa, and Natasha, who have traveled far to experience the condors with me, listened to countless stories, offered endless support, gloried in the program's successes, and consoled me whenever we lost condors.

And I thank Chad Olson, who has spent more hours talking with me about condors than anyone could possibly conceive. I thank him for his passion for condors, for his tireless support of my efforts, and for the extraordinary contributions he made to the Arizona condors during and beyond my time as Field Manager. I thank him for consoling me in my moments of grief for lost condors, for supporting me in moments of frustration and despair, and for rejoicing with me over small victories and large milestones. I thank him not only for understanding when my workday started at 4:00 AM and ended at 11:00 PM (or later on carcass-drop nights), but for all-too-often coming out in the field to help me or just to keep me company.

SUNSET AT THE GRAND CANYON. THE DAY DRAWS TO A CLOSE WITH A PROFOUNDLY QUIET RESONANCE. THE SUN DIPS OUT OF VIEW, CASTING A MUTED GLOW OVER A KALEIDOSCOPIC PALETTE OF REDS AND GREENS, GRAYS AND CREAMS. THE VASTNESS OF THE CANYON, THE TIMELESSNESS EXUDED BY ITS TOWERING ROCK WALLS, ITS PINNACLES AND DOMES, INSPIRE A REVERENT HUSH. SCORES OF VISITORS CROWD VIEWPOINTS ALONG THE RIM TRAIL, GAZING OUT OVER THE IMMENSE ABYSS, LOST IN REFLECTION, OR SPEAKING QUIETLY TO THEIR COMPANIONS. STEPS SLOW. SCHEDULES ARE FORSAKEN. SHADOWS LENGTHEN.

California condors often soar over the cliffs at Grand Canyon National Park's South Rim just before sunset and soon after sunrise. This condor displays the spread primaries, or outer wing feathers, that give these birds their striking flight profile.

Threading my way through the crowd lining the rim at Grand Canyon Village one such evening, I struggled to resist the canyon's breathless silence, the lure of that moment when day stands interminably still before rushing headlong into night. I was looking out for my charges and needed to make sure that they had settled down safely for the night. They were out of sight for the moment, expending a last bout of energy before succumbing to the inevitability of day's end. Glancing upward, I scanned the threads of pink and yellow-gold that streaked through the sky's fading blue. Within moments I saw what I was looking for. A huge black-and-white shadow materialized from an empty sky and headed toward me. I felt the usual prickle of adrenaline. Smiling to myself, I savored the moment for a brief second, knowing that an extraordinary sight would soon meet the assembled throngs.

Moments later, a California condor drifted into view above the crowd. And then another and another. Five in all, lined out like a squadron of military bombers. A palpable excitement washed over the crowd like a growing wave, gathering speed as it went. Some knew immediately that they were looking at highly endangered California condors. Others could not put a name to the magnificent sight that riveted their gaze and captured their imagination. All stood transfixed as the giant birds began diving, wheeling, circling, chasing. I knew the birds were just out for a typical evening flight before settling down to roost for the night, something they did most nights whether or not they had an audience. To the assembled crowd, though, the birds were putting on a show, engaging in a euphoric dance with each other, with the wind, with the sky.

And then, spontaneously, like the unexpected rumble of thunder on a clear day, the crowd began to clap. United by the beauty of the floating birds, awed by their grace and speed, overwhelmed by the uniqueness of what they were seeing, the onlookers responded as one, applauding the show, giving thanks for the performance of a lifetime. Nothing had been orchestrated, nothing planned. Yet wild birds going about their daily lives had united a large and disparate crowd and inspired them to cheer out loud. Moments later, the birds settled on the cliffs, people moved on to dinner, darkness settled on the canyon. As I left my charges and headed to my awaiting tent, I felt, as ever, grateful for my moments among condors and thankful for this place—Grand Canyon—that allowed so many to experience and appreciate a creature so utterly captivating, so highly treasured, so nearly lost.

It is almost inconceivable to anyone who has watched a condor floating with effortless grace over the vastness of the Grand Canyon that not so long ago only twenty-two of these birds existed worldwide. The condor's calamitous brush with extinction spawned an unprecedented recovery effort that began in the early 1980s and continues to this day. The Los Angeles Zoo and the San Diego Wild Animal Park initiated a captive-breeding program in 1982, using eggs, nestlings, and adults that were brought into captivity from the wild. But wild condor numbers continued their precipitous decline. Finally, in 1985, biologists made the decision to capture the last of the wild birds in order to ensure their safety and preserve their genetic material by incorporating them into a captive-breeding program. On Easter Sunday 1987, the last wild condor was captured, kenneled, and transported to his new zoo home. After thousands of years, the condor's great shadow no longer drifted over western landscapes.

Amidst dire prognostications for the condor's future, the captive-breeding program persisted, and, in 1992, the first captive-raised California condors were released into the wilds of California. Four years later, condors were also reintroduced to Arizona. It was not long before these condors, which were released from the Vermilion Cliffs in northern Arizona, discovered the nearby Grand Canyon, a place of limitless soaring, foraging, and nesting opportunities. The return of condors to the Grand Canyon area after an absence of at least seventy years has replaced a long-missing ecological piece in the canyon's historic ecosystem. It has also created an unprecedented opportunity for the public to easily view a spectacular, highly endangered creature in its own habitat.

This book chronicles the historical decline of the California condor and the efforts undertaken to save it. It travels the roller coaster of the California Condor Recovery Program's journey, touching on the events that have devastated it and the stunning successes that have uplifted it. The focus of this story is on Grand Canyon's condors—the condors that have been reintroduced in northern Arizona and have made the canyon their home. Yet the scope embraces many of the historic and current events in California, because the Arizona birds owe their history and their fates to the condors in California and to those who struggled to keep the California birds from extinction.

My own involvement with condors began in April 2000, when I came to Arizona for a month to help monitor the condors that had been released to the wild by the nonprofit group the Peregrine Fund. I returned that December to serve as field manager for the condor reintroduction effort in Arizona. Over the next four years, I monitored free-flying condors and cared for the captive flock awaiting release on the Vermilion Cliffs. I helped treat sick birds and teach young ones vital survival lessons. I released condors to the wild, documented their movements and activities, and recaptured those that needed attention. I watched over the Arizona condors with the anxiety, love, and pride of a parent, glorying in each of their successes, hurting for them in their failures, delighting in their individual personalities, and shaking my head at their antics. I was privileged to document the first egg laid in the wild since the beginning of the reintroduction program and to watch the first successful fledging of a wild-hatched chick. Throughout, I delighted in sharing the condors' story with an enthralled public.

Not so long ago, seeing a wild condor was impossible. Now, for the first time in decades, condors that have been raised in the wild can be seen soaring with their captive-raised and reintroduced counterparts over southern California's chaparral-covered hills and Arizona's Grand Canyon. Those Grand Canyon visitors who see condors leave the national park forever changed. I have seen people's faces light up with awe, wonder, and excitement as they watched condors drifting over their heads. I have answered innumerable excited questions about the condors' size, appearance, and personalities. I have seen people who never thought to distinguish between a raven and a vulture get caught up in the condor's story and become passionate advocates for their success. And I, like so many other visitors, have felt the breath catch in my throat as I watched a perched condor extend its giant wings and step into the wind.

This book is for the condors, which have made an indelible impression on the lives of so many.

1 THE NATURAL HISTORY OF CONDORS

"Those are the ugliest birds I've ever seen," exclaimed a gray-haired woman as she looked over the rim of the Grand Canyon at three California condors perched on a distant rock pedestal. It was not the first time I had heard those words expressed by a visitor to the canyon. It was even a sentiment I had once held myself. But as I looked down on the three condors whose activities I was monitoring that day, I did not see three ugly, naked-headed vultures. Instead, I saw three beloved individuals: Condors 176, 227, and 235. Condors 227 and 235 were goofing around, like typical condor adolescents: intertwining their necks and pushing at each other in a neck-wrestling match. Condor 176, meanwhile, studiously ignored the younger birds and gazed out over the canyon. I knew it would be only minutes before she launched herself into the sky. Condor 176 was not one to stay put for long.

California condors commonly fly with their legs and feet dangling. Exposing their legs to the breeze cools them and, in turn, reduces the condor's body temperature. The hanging legs may also produce drag to slow the condor's flight while the bird scans its surroundings for food or a safe perch.

Within six months of being released to the wild, captive-raised Condor 176 had journeyed hundreds of miles and explored parts of four states. As a two-year-old, she proved that reintroduced condors could be self-sufficient by finding her own food for months at a time.

She had always been like that. Long after the other condors in her captive-raised cohort (a group of same-aged juvenile condors released to the wild together) had settled down for the night on Arizona's Hurricane Cliffs, Condor 176 would keep flying.

"She was constantly in the air," then field manager of the reintroduction project, Shawn Farry, recalls. "She would fly endless figure-eights over the release site right up until dark."

While other condors seemed content to lounge on the cliffs, preening or resting or playing with other condors, 176 seemed driven to fly. By the time she had been in the wild a mere six months, Condor 176 had explored parts of four states, flying to Mesa Verde National Park in Colorado (a round-trip flight of approximately four hundred miles [650 km]), to the environs of Las Vegas, Nevada, and to Milford, Utah (both round-trip journeys of approximately two hundred miles [325 km]). And these were just the trips Farry and his field crew were able to document.

Finally, as a two-year-old (still a juvenile for a species that does not reach maturity until the age of five or six), 176 left the release area one day in the early fall of 2000 and disappeared. Despite the two radio transmitters she wore on her wings to help biologists track her daily movements, she could not be found. Although we did not like to admit it, over the ensuing months most of us gave up hope she would ever be seen again.

And then, one afternoon in January 2001, more than three months after her disappearance, we received a phone call. The caller reported seeing a condor at Toroweap, a remote area on the North Rim of the Grand Canyon, two days earlier. There was a big number "76" on each of her wings, the tourist claimed. Every reintroduced condor wears a numbered tag on each wing. Condor 176's black tags were painted with the white number "76" on them. It had to be her.

Minutes later, Chad Olson, a fellow biologist, and I were throwing camping gear into our work truck and, soon after, began an epic night journey from the small outpost at the Vermilion Cliffs where we were based to Toroweap. The last sixty miles (97 km) of what was usually a three-hour journey was on a snow-covered dirt road that had become almost impassable in the blizzard that raged around us. We finally arrived at the Toroweap campground at 1:00 AM. Quickly, we extricated our radio-tracking equipment and held the antenna over the rim of the sheer 3,000-foot (900-m) cliff that dropped away in front of us. A faint, "blip, blip, blip" greeted our ears. It was 176's radio transmitters, emitting signals from a spot on the cliff far below us. Condor 176 was alive.

We were up at dawn the next day, eager to get a look at her. When the sun began warming the large boulders strewn along the cliff's rim, 176 took to the skies and soared into view, her magnificent nine-foot (3-m) wingspan casting a broad shadow on the cliff wall as she crossed over the Colorado River to the west. For hours we watched her fly, treating ourselves to the sight of an individual neither of us had seen before. She captured both our imaginations and our hearts on that day, embodying everything that epitomizes a truly wild condor. Eventually, satisfied that she was not only alive, but thriving, Olson and I headed for home.

It was well over a month before we saw her again. Over time, Condor 176 became less elusive as she began to consort with condors that frequented less remote haunts. Periodically, though, she disappeared for weeks at a time, returning to the remotest corners of the Grand Canyon and southern Utah. Her disappearances no longer gave us cause for concern. More than any other Arizona condor, 176 could take care of herself.

⁓

As I watched Condor 176 perched next to Condors 227 and 235, I felt lucky, as I always did when in her presence, to see her on one of her rare departures from the sky. Suddenly, without effort, she extended her great wings and stepped into the wind.

"Oh my God," the gray-haired woman standing at my side, exclaimed. "That's the most beautiful thing I've ever seen!" I smiled to myself. As homely as a condor might look when perched, there are few sights in nature that rival the dream-like, floating beauty of a condor in flight. The woman glanced toward others gathered nearby, trying to make sure that everyone was appreciating the astonishingly beautiful sight of Condor 176 drifting over our heads. And then the questions started. Another visitor to the Grand Canyon had been hooked.

Condor Size, Taxonomy, and Habits

California condors are the largest flying land birds in North America. With a wingspan of approximately nine feet (3 m), they dwarf golden and bald eagles, which have wingspans of about seven feet (2 m). Whereas a bald eagle (*Haliaeetus leucocephalus*) weighs on average ten pounds (4.5 kg), California condors typically weigh between sixteen and twenty-four pounds (7–11 kg).

Condors are the largest vultures in the New World Vulture family (Cathartidae). There are two species of condors in this family, the California condor (*Gymnogyps californianus*) in North America and the Andean condor (*Vultur gryphus*), which has a wingspan longer than ten feet (3 m) and lives in South America. Interestingly, although California condors are closely related to the other six vulture species in the Americas (Andean condor, black vulture [*Coragyps atratus*], turkey vulture [*Cathartes aura*], king vulture [*Sarcoramphus papa*], greater yellow-headed vulture [*Cathartes melambrotus*], and lesser yellow-headed vulture [*Cathartes burrovianus*]), they are not closely related to vultures in other parts of the world. Rather, based on anatomical, morphological (structural), behavioral, and molecular evidence, the New World Vultures' closest relatives are the storks (Ciconiidae). Vultures in the New and Old World families have evolved to fill a similar ecological niche as soaring scavengers, yet they are not closely related. Instead, their superficial similarities are the result of convergent evolution, the development of similar attributes (such as large wings, and featherless heads and necks) needed to make a living in a particular way.

Furthermore, while the Old World Vultures (Accipitridae) of Europe and Asia are closely related to raptors (birds of prey), North and South American vultures are not. Unlike raptors and Old World Vultures, New World Vultures do not have a functional hind toe or an internal separation of the nostrils. The latter makes it possible to look through one of a New World Vulture's nostrils and see out the other.

Most of the characteristics shared by New World Vultures and storks—similarities in their skeletal structure, their skull formation, and the arrangement of some of their musculature—are imperceptible to the casual observer. One very visible exception is an inflatable air sac in the necks of California condors and storks that plays a role in courtship displays. New World Vultures also share some behavioral traits with their stork relatives. The best known of such traits is the use of urohydrosis to help themselves thermoregulate, or maintain a comfortable temperature, in hot weather. When urohydrating, condors and their relatives deliberately dribble urinary waste onto their legs. As the fluid evaporates, the legs are cooled and, subsequently, cool blood from the leg area circulates to other regions of the body, bringing down the bird's body temperature. Because of urohydration, condors' legs are typically a chalky white color, a byproduct of the wastes deposited on their

Like all vultures in North and South America, this turkey vulture has perforated nostrils. This trait is one of several that distinguish these vultures from the unrelated but similar looking European, Asian, and African vultures.

normally gray legs. Old World Vultures do not urohydrate, and this behavioral trait is a primary distinction between New and Old World Vultures.

Condor Diet and Food-Finding Abilities

California condors are scavengers that feed exclusively on carrion. Unlike raptors, to which they bear a superficial similarity, condors do not have bills or talons designed for killing animals. Instead, condors have blunt toenails and feet that have evolved for walking. Condors use their strong legs and large feet as leverage when standing on a carcass, so they can more easily tear off meat. Their powerful bills can tear open a carcass's tough hide, pull out the available meat, and break small bones such as ribs. Rasp-like projections on their tongues help condors hold onto soft, slippery innards. Like vultures around the world, condors have evolved a featherless head and neck that helps them thermoregulate, and allows them to penetrate openings in a carcass and extricate innards without excessively soiling their feathers. Despite this adaptation, condors are fanatics about keeping clean and often fly to a water source to bathe soon after feeding.

Condors typically feed on medium-to-large mammal carcasses such as elk, mule deer, and cattle, although they are opportunistic and will feed on virtually any dead animals they can find. Biologists working on the reintroduction program in Arizona have documented condors' feeding on dead squirrels, porcupines, ducks, fish, coyotes, foxes, bobcats, mountain lions, bighorn sheep, domestic sheep, dogs, cattle, horses, and mules. Scientists have seen condors on the coast of California feeding on the remnants of marine mammals such as sea lions and whales. Other menu items for the condors in California have included ground squirrels, kangaroo rats, jackrabbits, and wild pigs. Although condors prefer freshly dead animals, they are able to ingest putrid meat if no other food is available. Like their close relative the turkey vulture, condors appear to be able to withstand exponentially higher levels of toxins such as botulism and salmonella than most other birds.

Unlike turkey vultures, which use their highly developed sense of smell (an anomalous trait in the bird world) to find dead animals, condors are visual scavengers. They use their exceptional vision to locate carcasses. Although capable of finding food on their own, condors typically watch the activities of other scavengers, such as turkey vultures, common ravens (*Corvus corax*), and eagles. These scavengers are conspicuous when assembling at a carcass, and condors are quick to hone in on their activities and follow them to the food source. Their larger size usually allows condors to easily usurp a carcass. Although smaller scavengers may lose out on some meat by having their carcass taken over by the larger condor, they may also benefit by gaining access to the meat in larger animals with tough hides that can only be torn open by the condor's powerful bill.

Carrion is a widely dispersed, ephemeral, and unpredictable food source. As a result, condors at a carcass ingest as much meat as they can hold in their crops, an enlargement of the esophagus that functions as a temporary food storage area. A condor's crop can hold more than three pounds (1.5 kg) of meat, which the bird will digest over a period of about twenty-four hours. Condors will feed every two to three days if food is available, but they can survive for more than two weeks without feeding.

Breast feathers parted by a distended crop (an enlargement of the esophagus) indicate that this condor has fed recently. Adult condors have pink heads and a correspondingly pink crop, whereas juveniles have a black crop that is less discernible against their black feathers.

How California Condors Are Numbered and Marked

Few species exist in which every individual is known, marked, and accounted for. In the case of California condors, every individual alive or dead since about 1976 has been catalogued in the California Condor Studbook, which resides at the San Diego Wild Animal Park. Each condor is given a studbook number based on the date that it hatched. In addition, the studbook keeper records each bird's sex, parentage, hatch date, release date, and whether it's alive or dead. As a condor hatches, biologists give it the next sequential studbook number. They later mark the condor with identifying wing tags.

The first condor listed in the studbook (Condor 1) is known as Topa Topa, a male hatched in 1966. Brought into captivity when he was less than a year old due to an injury, Topa

All condors carry unique identifying wing tags to help biologists monitor them in the wild. The vinyl tag folds over the wing, allowing the number to be read whether the bird is flying or perched. Female Condor 119 wears tag number 19.

(as he is fondly called by his keepers) was the only California condor in captivity between 1967 and 1982. Topa still resides at the Los Angeles Zoo, where he continues to father new condors for release back into the wild.

Currently, the oldest condor in Arizona is Condor 119, which hatched at the San Diego Wild Animal Park on March 15, 1995. Captive condors that are released to the wild wear identifying wing markers so researchers can monitor them and track their activities. Because field biologists often need to read the reintroduced condor's wing markers at distances of a mile or more, the tags are large and contain no more than two conspicuous identifying numbers. Typically, the last two digits of a condor's studbook number are marked on the condor's wing tags. Condor 119, therefore, wears wing tag number "19." Her mate, Condor 122, wears tag number "22," and so on. As biologists have released increasing numbers of condors to the wild in Arizona, this simple numbering system has become, of necessity, more complex. When confronted with having Condors 123 and 223 in the same population, for example, biologists chose to leave "23" on the older bird's tags and use a simple "3"—the last number of Condor 223's studbook number—for the younger bird's tags. With more and more condors surviving and reproducing, devising suitable tag numbers has become more challenging, but this is a problem everyone involved in the reintroduction program welcomes.

Many visitors to Grand Canyon stare out over a vast and seemingly empty landscape and cannot conceive that sufficient dead animals exist to feed a lone coyote, let alone a contingent of ravens, turkey vultures, California condors, and other scavengers. Yet the canyon's seeming dearth of life is, in part, a trick of scale. If one looks through binoculars, what looks like a dry, empty landscape comes to life, revealing bighorn sheep on a cliff ledge, rock squirrels darting to and fro, and ravens wheeling around in the sky. The canyon and its environs teem with wildlife. And to the condors' benefit, many animals succumb to heat, drought, falls off cliffs, sickness,

Condors may fly hundreds of miles in a day, reaching altitudes as high as 15,000 feet (4,600 m), although they usually fly about 500 feet (150 m) above the ground.

battles with other animals, predators, and fatal encounters with moving vehicles.

If no dead animals are available nearby, California condors fly farther afield in search of food. Condors that find a meal at the South Rim one day may find their next meal outside Zion National Park in southern Utah the next. Supremely adapted for soaring and gliding, condors can fly for hours on end without flapping their wings and without expending much energy. Condors may fly hundreds of miles in a day, reaching altitudes as high as 15,000 feet (4,600 m), although they usually fly about 500 feet (150 m) above the ground.

Condor Personalities

Watching Condors 227 and 235, I smiled as they began neck-wrestling again. Condor 227 has always searched out playful fellow condors. If he arrived somewhere where no condors were congregated, he would hightail it to the next place he thought he might find his compadres. Distance was never an impediment to Condor 227. He once flew more than seventy-five miles (120 km) in the space of a few hours in search of other condors. On another occasion, he showed us that he could travel at least fifty miles per hour (80 kph) while making a typical flight between the release area and the South Rim.

Despite being a spectacular flier of proven prowess, 227 also showed us that even apparently skilled young condors can miscalculate and get into situations that more experienced birds would avoid. One day in June 2002, after spending several hours playing on a beach next to the Colorado River, 227 flapped laboriously into the sky, intent on moving to the other side of the river. The wind that day was ferocious.

Watching from Navajo Bridge, several hundred feet above Condor 227, field biologist Kate

Parmentier held tight to the railing as she felt the bridge swaying under her feet. Almost blinded by the wind, she looked down on 227 as he began to cross the river. And suddenly, she felt her heart jump into her throat as she watched him stall midway across. Flapping hard, 227 hung over the river, no longer moving forward despite his efforts. And then, unexpectedly, he tumbled into the swift-moving water. Parmentier watched helplessly from above as the only visible part of 227—his head—bobbed downstream. Quickly, 227 began using his

Like all condors, each had a **unique personality,** individualized traits, and their own personal history.

massive wings to pull himself to shore, but the relentless current carried him away. The young condor struggled on, rowing with his wings, his head barely remaining above water.

After what felt like an eternity to Parmentier, 227 finally escaped the current and moved into slower-moving water. He was soon dragging himself up onto the beach. He shook himself off and then spread his wings nonchalantly to dry himself out. "I thought we were going to lose him for sure," Parmentier later told me, "but 227 is an *amazing* condor!" Condor 227 likely learned an important lesson about how to handle gusty wind conditions that day—one of the many lessons a young condor has to learn in order to become self-sufficient.

California condors are intelligent, curious birds that learn a host of survival skills before reaching maturity. Unlike hawks and falcons, condors are not preprogrammed to instinctively know how to find food and to survive on their own. Young, captive-raised falcons that are released to the wild at an early age teach themselves to hunt and can be independent of their human caretakers in a few weeks time. Condors, on the other hand, may take months to learn to find food on their own, to take advantage of invisible breaths of wind to soar on seemingly windless days, to avoid predators on the ground and in the sky, and to satisfy their curiosity without endangering themselves in the increasingly developed world in which they live.

After several minutes of neck-wrestling, Condor 227 managed to push Condor 235 off the rock pinnacle. Effortlessly, 235 opened her wings and floated just out of 227's reach. Seconds later, Condor 227 took off after her, and the two young condors drifted over to another perch. To an onlooker, the two birds likely seemed identical, distinguishable only by the large numbered tags affixed to their wings. Having watched over them since before they took their first flight as wild birds, however, they were as different to me as two siblings are to their parents. Like all condors, each had a unique personality, individualized traits, and their own personal history. Those of us who worked on the reintroduction and monitoring of condors in Arizona know each bird's character, and had either witnessed or heard about its trials and tribulations, its adventures and misadventures.

Condor 235 was the youngest of her release cohort when she flew free for the first time at the Vermilion Cliffs release area on December 29, 2000. Although female and male condors look identical, females are generally subordinate to males of the same age. In addition, younger condors are usually less dominant than older condors. But 235 seemed oblivious to these "rules."

Newly released condors are fed supplementary food at the release site, and the older birds take advantage of this free food as well, particularly in the winter. Carcasses are placed on the cliff rim at night, when the birds are sleeping soundly on the cliff face, so that the condors do not see food being provided to them by their human caretakers. Field biologists watch newly released condors carefully to ensure they are competing successfully with the older birds to access food.

Typically, young condors arrive at the carcasses early, and they begin feeding immediately to ingest as much as they can before the more-dominant older birds arrive and commandeer the food. But 235 was anything but typical. Bundled up against the bitter cold, I would watch the condor flock feeding (from a discrete observation blind) and wonder when 235 was going to show up. Almost invariably, she was the last condor to arrive at the feeding frenzy. By then, juveniles stood around the

Like Condor 176, Condor 235 had an independent streak and a knack for eluding the field crew by disappearing into inaccessible or remote areas.

carcasses, sneaking in occasionally for a quick bite, while the dominant adults fed aggressively. Finally, Condor 235 would fly in, and instead of taking her place with the other juveniles, she would land right on top of a carcass, spreading her wings over as much of it as she could in a very atypical pose for a condor. Perhaps her astonishing behavior gave the adults enough pause for her to get in a good meal. However she did it, 235 always managed to stuff her crop so full that it looked like she had swallowed a basketball.

Like Condor 176, Condor 235 had an independent streak and a knack for eluding the field crew by disappearing into inaccessible or remote areas. She quickly learned to key in on the activities of turkey vultures, and she was the first of her cohort to find and feed on a non-proffered (not supplied by field crewmembers) carcass. Despite being a great flier and carcass-finder, Condor 235 was endearingly clumsy at landings. On countless occasions, hidden in our observation blind atop the cliffs, we watched 235 fly gracefully over the rim, flare her wings, touch down, and then, inevitably, face-plant on her bill. Years after her release to the wild, I could still reliably identify 235 by her comical landings.

Female Condor 119 soars over Grand Canyon Village. Her white underwing feathers, colorful pink and yellow head, and red eye indicate that she is an adult.

Condor Maturation, Coloration, and Reproduction

As I continued to watch Condors 227 and 235, a third condor materialized, as though borne of the winds that permeate the canyon. Gliding toward the two black-headed youngsters, Condor 123 flared his wings and touched down softly onto the pinnacle. Condor 235 immediately lunged at him with a slightly open bill, the typical response of a subordinate condor to a dominant one. Seconds later, she ceded her perch to 123, whose pink and yellow head marked him as an adult, then opened her wings and drifted away from the pinnacle. Condor 227 was quick to follow.

Like other large birds, California condors are slow to reach maturity. As newly hatched nestlings, condors are covered in a soft, white down, but they have a featherless grayish-yellow head, neck, wings, and crop area. Within twenty to twenty-nine days, a woollier, dark-grayish down begins to push out and replace the white natal down. By the age of fifty days, nestling condors are fully covered by this short grayish down, including parts of their head and neck areas. At approximately two months of age, condors begin growing their familiar black body and flight feathers. While this juvenile body plumage is nearly complete at the age of twenty-three to twenty-four weeks, the flight feathers and underwing feathers continue growing until the condors are about six months old. At around this age, nestling condors fledge (leave the nest for the first time). Although the skin on the head and neck of newly fledged condors is black, and the head looks featherless at a distance, the top of the head and back of the neck are covered in a thin layer of fuzzy, gray down that the condors will retain until they are about two years old. Nestling and juvenile condors have dark brown irises and dark bills.

After two years of age, condors' eyes transition to the deep red color that they will retain as adults. At three years of age, condors develop a pink ring around their still-black neck; gradually the rest of the neck and head will turn pink as well. As four-year-olds, condors have a blotchy black and pink face. The pink on the face usually develops first around the bill, eyes, and ear openings, then spreads to the rest of the face. By five or six years of age, depending on the individual, condors have the pink and yellow heads that are characteristic of adults. Their dark bill also begins to turn ivory in color, completing their adult appearance.

Juvenile and adult condors also differ in their plumage. Juvenile condors have a triangular patch of smudgy-gray feathers on their underwings. These gray feathers will gradually be replaced with white feathers as the condor ages. By the time a condor reaches adulthood, its underwing feathers will be a pure white, providing the sharply contrasting black-and-white underwing that is characteristic of California condors. Meanwhile, the dark brown or black secondary flight feathers on the inner portions

The smoky-gray coloration of this condor's underwing marks it as a juvenile, as does its black head and dark eye.

The Transformation from Juvenile to Adult

1. Condor 305 during his first year. Until about the age of two, a juvenile condor has a black head and bill, dark eye, and a covering of dense, gray down on its head and neck.

2. Condor 223 at the age of three. After condors reach two years of age, the skin on their necks begins to turn pink, earning three-year-olds the moniker "ringnecks." At this age, their eyes begin to lighten and the membrane encircling each eye turns red. A condor's ability to inflate its neck develops with age and serves as a sign of dominance.

3. Condor 193 at the age of five. Four- and five-year-old condors typically have a blotchy appearance with their formerly black face becoming mottled with pinks and yellows. Condors develop at different rates, with some five-year-olds showing fully pink heads and others retaining their freckled appearance.

4. Condor 123 at the age of six. Adult condors are surprisingly colorful, with their head and neck colors becoming even more vibrant during courtship displays or agonistic interactions. The back of their neck is typically a purplish blue, while the front is pink. Their heads are a mixture of orange, pink, and yellow. As Condor 123 ages, he will lose the black spots on his face, his eye will become a deeper red, and his bill will attain an ivory color.

of juveniles' wings are gradually replaced by gray feathers in adulthood.

No one knows exactly how long condors may live. The oldest known condor died at the National Zoo in Washington, D.C., at the age of forty-five years, but given the longevity of the closely related Andean condor, biologists suspect that wild California condors could live as long as seventy years. As with other long-lived creatures, condors not only mature slowly but have a very slow reproductive rate. Although reintroduced condors in California have begun reproducing as young as five years of age, condors typically do not begin breeding until age six to eight years. Biologists believe that most condors pair and mate for life, but studies confirming this remain inconclusive. Although several young, captive-raised pairs are known to have split up after their first nesting attempt, most condors do appear to stay with their chosen mate until one of them dies. Regardless of the longevity of condor pairs, all condors are monogamous during each breeding attempt.

Condors nest in caves or other large crevices. A pair in California in the 1980s repeatedly used an enormous cavity high up in a sequoia. In Arizona, trees with cavities large enough to support condors are nonexistent, but cave sites in cliffs are limitless. Unlike the Old World Vultures, condors and other New World Vultures do not build stick nests. Instead, they lay their eggs on the floor of sheltered locations such as caves, hollow logs, or stumps. In the case of condors, the female typically lays her egg directly on the floor of a cave. Prior to laying, the pair will smooth the surface (a process known as nest grooming) and sometimes form a slight depression in the bottom of the cave using their bills. Once the pair has selected and readied their cave, and the female has laid her single large, white egg (approximately five inches [13 cm] in length), both parents share incubation duties. Incubation typically lasts fifty-seven days. It takes almost three days for a condor to hatch. The condor chick's exodus from its egg begins with a process known as pipping, in which the encased chick creates a crack along the more pointed end of the egg by tapping at the eggshell with a temporary projection on its bill known as an egg tooth. The hatching is complete when the egg cracks open and the condor hatchling emerges.

Nestling condors are fed regurgitated meat by both of their parents. Although the nestling will leave the nest and take its first flight at around six months of age, it remains dependent on its parents for food for as long as a year. Because of the long nestling and post-fledging dependency period, a breeding attempt typically lasts more than a year. As a rule, condors that raise their one offspring successfully usually do not re-nest the following breeding season. Instead, they produce one offspring every other year. This low reproductive rate contributed substantially to the condor's slow recovery after their numbers were depleted.

One evening in June 2001, I walked along the Rim Trail west of Grand Canyon Village in search of condors that I had tracked to the area using radiotelemetry. As I came around a corner, the vast canyon stood before me with its spires and columns, its looming walls and colorful turrets, aflame in the setting sun. On a rock pinnacle in the foreground, a perched condor, elegant in dress-black, looked out over the canyon toward the Colorado River far below. Condor 114 serenely surveyed his vast realm in a timeless portrait, a scene that had played itself over and over for thousands of years. I felt as though I had stepped into the Pleistocene.

Condors have graced western skies for thousands of years. Recently, they have led a precarious existence, with only twenty-two remaining at the population's low point in 1982.

Condors in the Pleistocene

More than ten thousand years ago, the passage of a California condor's great shadow over the castellated buttes and the sheer cliffs of Grand Canyon was likely a common sight. During the Pleistocene epoch (approximately 1.8 million to 10,000 years ago), the canyon and its environs were slightly wetter and cooler. Between about 30,000 and 8,500 years ago, the Inner Gorge was dominated by juniper (*Juniperus* sp.) woodlands growing alongside scattered desert plants that are typical of today's Mohave Desert. The surrounding plateau was comprised of grasslands and montane forests.

A surprisingly diverse complement of large animals lived in the region. Herds of massive Columbian mammoths (*Mammuthus columbi*) grazed on a variety of grasses, sedges, and other plants on the plateaus. Small, burro-like horses (*Equus* sp.) and shrub oxen (*Euceratherium collinum*), which looked like a cross between cattle and sheep, foraged in and around the canyon. Large single-humped camels (*Camelops hesternus*) and bison (*Bison* sp.) roamed the rims and adjacent plateaus, and they may also have ventured into the more accessible regions of the inner canyon. The enormous Shasta ground sloth (*Nothrotheriops shastensis*), which stood about six feet (2 m) tall and weighed more than three hundred pounds (135 kg), fed on desert globemallow (*Sphaeralcea ambigua*) and Mormon tea (*Ephedra nevadensis*), and retreated to large canyon caves for shelter. The Harrington's mountain goat (*Oreamnos harringtoni*), the most common large mammal in the canyon, clambered around on the cliffs and browsed along the streambanks, while the yellow-bellied marmot (*Marmota flaviventris*) made its whistling alarm call from boulder-strewn slopes. Familiar predators like the mountain lion (*Felis concolor*) stalked this herbivorous bounty. And *Gymnogyps californianus*, the bird we now call the California condor, patrolled the skies, searching for the dead animals that made up its diet.

The fossil history of the California condor dates back to the late Pleistocene. Condors first appear in the Grand Canyon fossil record more than 43,000 years ago. Evidence of the prehistoric presence of the now-common turkey vulture is scarce, but condors did appear to share the canyon with the black vulture, a species that today is widespread in the southeast and ranges as far West as southern Arizona. Condors and black vultures may have been accompanied by a scavenger that dwarfed even the condor. Fifteen-thousand-year-old fossils of a large carrion feeder known as Merriam's teratorn (*Teratornis merriami*), which had a wingspan as large as twelve feet (3.7 m), have been found in Stantons Cave in the Marble Canyon area of Grand Canyon National Park. The bones of condors, black vultures, and the animals on which they once fed

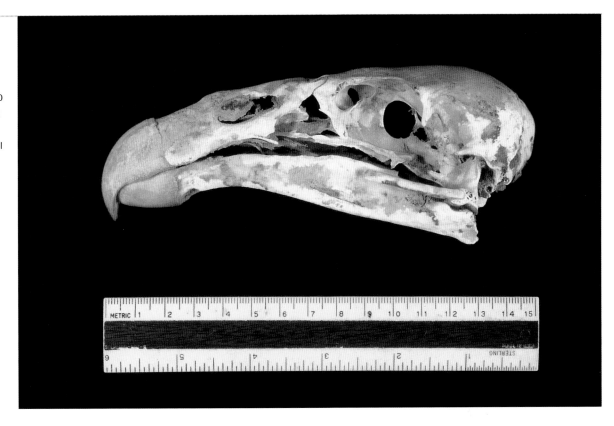

Researchers were astonished when tests revealed that this beautifully preserved condor skull, found in a remote cave in Grand Canyon, was 12,000 years old. The bits of skin still attached to the skull and the presence of the keratinous bill had led them to believe that it belonged to a more recent resident of the canyon.

have been found in numerous Redwall Limestone caves throughout the Grand Canyon. Many of these bones have been preserved in ancient woodrat (also known as packrat) middens. Woodrats (*Neotoma* spp.) will collect any objects they can carry and will cache a variety of plant and animal matter in their nests. Over time, these treasures become glued together by the woodrat's urine, and in dry locations such middens may last for thousands of years.

Condor bones have also been found in caves preserved amidst Shasta ground sloth dung, fossilized in ringtail (*Bassariscus astutus*) refuse deposits, and lying on or just under the cave substrate surface.

Perhaps the finest ancient condor specimen discovered in a Grand Canyon cave was a well-preserved, perfectly intact condor skull found in Marble Canyon's Stevens Cave by paleontologist Steven Emslie. Dried skin and the keratinous bill

Captain Meriwether Lewis dedicated nearly three pages of an 1806 journal entry to a detailed description of a California condor, wounded and taken alive by a member of his exploration party. Lewis speculated that it was "the largest bird of North America . . . it weighed 25 lbs . . . [and] between the extremities of the wings it measured 9 feet 2 inches."

remained on the skull. Amazingly, radiocarbon dating showed the skull to be 12,000 years old. To date, only a miniscule fraction of the Grand Canyon's caves has been explored, and virtually all of these are within the Inner Gorge. Caves higher up in the canyon's walls, which would have been easier for condors to access because of stronger winds and greater uplift, have yet to be comprehensively examined.

The diverse megafauna that thrived in the Grand Canyon for thousands of years during the Pleistocene epoch began to dwindle with the ending of the last ice age. As glaciers retreated from the higher mountains of the Colorado Plateau and from almost all of the northern regions of the continent between 12,000 and 9,000 years ago, the climate warmed and dried, and seasonal temperature fluctuations became more extreme. As the climate changed, the ranges of certain plants shifted upslope as the plants sought to maintain the moisture they needed. Over time, desert plants replaced juniper woodlands in the Inner Gorge, while junipers and other woody plants now grew successfully only on the cooler rims and upper reaches of the canyon. Animals also moved northward to cooler climes and more suitable habitat. By 8,500 years ago, the inner canyon had been transformed from a woodland habitat to today's Mohave and Sonoran deserts and their associated riparian biotic communities.

This change in climate and vegetation communities coincided with the mass extinction of the Pleistocene megafauna. Over a relatively short time, individual species blinked out, leaving only bone fragments. Merriam's teratorns, Columbian mammoths, camels, the small horses, Harrington's mountain goats, and Shasta ground sloths all became extinct during this period.

Why the Pleistocene megafauna died off remains a mystery. One hypothesis is that the postglacial climate change made the canyon and other areas unsuitable for these large animals (and for many smaller animals like the yellow-bellied marmot). Another is that unsustainable hunting pressure from humans, whose signs first appear in the archaeological record of the Colorado Plateau about 11,000 to 12,000 years ago, led ultimately to the extinctions.

Range Contraction and Historic Accounts

Whatever the reason for the extinction of the Pleistocene megafauna, its demise had a drastic effect on the condor's range. During the Pleistocene, the California condor's range formed a large U-shaped swath around North America. Beginning as far north as British Columbia, it extended south through Oregon and California to Baja California in Mexico, then east through Texas

> Over a relatively short time, individual species blinked out, leaving only bone fragments.

and across to Florida. Fossilized condor bones found in a boreal bog deposit in upper New York State provide the most northeasterly evidence of the condor's range.

As the animals that comprised the condor's diet disappeared, condors must have found it harder to find food, and, over time, their populations dwindled. By historic times, condors were confined to western North America. Condors may have survived in coastal areas by feeding on the large marine mammals that washed onto beaches and on the abundant salmon that died along coastal waterways after spawning. A California condor was shot by a

CURRENT AND HISTORIC RANGE
OF CALIFORNIA CONDORS

Current Range of the
California Condor

● Sites where remains of prehistoric
California condors have been found

member of the Lewis and Clark expedition as the bird gorged on dead fish near the mouth of the Columbia River (between present-day Oregon and Washington) in November 1805. Meriwether Lewis detailed another condor that was shot and wounded by his party in a journal entry dated February 17, 1806. Based on incidental reports, condors ranged as far inland as Alberta, Idaho, Montana, Utah, and Arizona. By the 1940s, however, the condor's range did not extend beyond southern California.

Condors lived in Arizona until the early 1920s. However, whether condors occupied the Grand Canyon region and other parts of Arizona continuously from the Pleistocene to the early twentieth century, or whether condors were gone from this region by the end of the Pleistocene and dispersing birds from California then re-colonized the area in the 1800s, remains much debated. Steven Emslie, the avian paleontologist responsible for many of the condor bone discoveries in Grand Canyon caves, found no bones younger than 9,750 years old. The age of the condor bones he examined coincided with the Pleistocene extinctions, leading him to believe that the Arizona condors disappeared from the area along with the rest of the Grand Canyon Pleistocene megafauna. According to Emslie and others, condors may have returned to Arizona after large herds of horses, cattle, and sheep, introduced to the West in the 1700s, provided a new food source.

Although no condor bones from historical times have been found in the Grand Canyon, other condor experts remain convinced that the canyon could well have harbored a vestigial population of condors from the Pleistocene until 1924, when the last condor documented in Arizona was seen near Williams, sixty miles (100 km) south of the national park. Considering that, in 2003, numerous hikers camped in the drainage below the nest site of the first successful nesting pair of reintroduced condors in the canyon and did not notice their activities, it is quite possible that condors persisted in the canyon unseen.

Whether or not condors had a *continuous* presence in Grand Canyon between the Pleistocene and historic times, evidence suggests they did occur in small numbers in Arizona in the 1800s and early 1900s. On March 26, 1885, Edgar Mearns, an ornithologist and U.S. Army surgeon, spotted a condor feeding on a dead horse alongside numerous ravens between Ash Creek and Bumble Bee, in southern Yavapai County. Another ornithologist, Elliott Coues, documented "several individuals" at Fort Yuma in September 1865 and claimed that California condors were resident in southern Arizona. A rancher named Jack Alwinkle, who had spent several years in California and was familiar with condors, claimed to have shot one around 1890 near the summit of Mount Lemmon in southeastern

Nevertheless, even the remoteness of the Grand Canyon region could not protect the condor. ∝

Arizona's Santa Catalina Mountains. He used the bird, which was perched on a rock "some distance" from their camp, to test the range on his rifle; he described it as being twice as large as a turkey vulture and the only one of its kind he had seen since leaving California.

The validity of these reports has been questioned by some ornithologists. However, two reports from the vicinity of the Grand Canyon have met with greater acceptance from the scientific community. One of these occurred at Pierce Ferry on the western edge of today's Grand Canyon National Park in March 1881. After crossing the Colorado River at Pierce Ferry, three men, Bill Johnson, Joe Henderson, and Miles Noyes, camped under the Grand Wash Cliffs. While breakfasting the following morning, the men observed what they first mistook for two people on top of a distant cliff. A more careful examination showed that two large vultures were perched there. The birds took off shortly thereafter and flew directly over the men's camp. One of the men hurriedly shot at one of the birds, breaking its right wing. Tumbling out of the sky, the bird fell heavily onto some large boulders and was killed. The men measured the ill-fated bird with their gun and

found that it was over a gun length in height and had a wingspan of more than three gun lengths.

In 1924, an ornithologist named Edouard Jacot observed a condor and some golden eagles feeding on a carcass near Williams. Jacot's sighting was the last time a condor was seen in Arizona before the reintroductions began in 1996. While tantalizingly fragmentary, the proximity of these last two sightings to the Grand Canyon lend support to the idea that condors existed in this area throughout historic times. Nevertheless, even the remoteness of the Grand Canyon region could not protect the condor.

The California condor is often referred to as a "relict" of the Pleistocene and has been said to be a "species with one foot and even one wing in the grave."[1] Because condors appear to have depended on the carcasses of Pleistocene megafauna, many assume that the demise of these animals naturally relegated the condor to a similar fate. That the extinction of the Pleistocene megafauna affected condors seems indisputable. However, condors are exceptionally opportunistic feeders and flexible in their habitat requirements—traits that do not typically lead to extinction. Like other species that lived in the West during the Pleistocene and thrive to this day, the condor should be considered a Pleistocene survivor, not an aged member of a tired evolutionary line. Were it not for hundreds of years of human

[1] Loye H. Miller, "Succession in the Cathartine Dynasty," *Condor* 44 (1942): 213.

During the Pleistocene, condors in Arizona fed on animals such as mammoths and shrub oxen. Today, condors still find abundant food in the Grand Canyon region. This reintroduced condor found and fed on two elk carcasses and one mule deer carcass in a single day.

persecution coupled with an extraordinarily low reproductive rate, condors would likely still be thriving, and their relevance in today's world would never have been questioned.

Persecution and Poisoning

Most likely, condors were never overly abundant, although their tendency to travel widely and convene at carcasses may have made them appear more numerous than they actually were to some early naturalists. Throughout the 1900s, however, condor populations declined precipitously because of both indirect and direct human persecution.

According to Lloyd Kiff, a former leader of the California Condor Recovery Team, an advisory board for the recovery of California condors in North America, "It appears that the bird was doing quite well on the Pacific Coast from British Columbia south to northern Baja until the 1790s, when Europeans arrived and started shooting it. Throughout the late eighteenth century and the nineteenth century, virtually every account of the California condor includes a description of how the birds were killed. Everybody shot condors."[2]

Whether it was because condors were erroneously considered a threat to livestock, because they were shot as scientific specimens and for museum collections, or merely because they made an appealingly large target, condors were killed indiscriminately and in great numbers. Early miners shot condors to use their large feather quills as receptacles for holding gold dust. Several American Indian tribes in California killed condors for ceremonial purposes.

Early predator-poisoning campaigns also decimated condor populations. Efforts to kill grizzly bears, wolves, and coyotes using strychnine- and cyanide-laced carcasses inadvertently targeted scavengers, which were drawn to these readily available meals.

In the 1980s, the first studies of condors using radiotelemetry to track the birds' movements led to the discovery of an even more insidious means of poisoning and perhaps the greatest threat to condors past and present: lead. Necropsies of three condors showed that the birds had ingested lead bullet fragments after feeding on deer entrails left in the field by hunters or on deer killed by hunters but never retrieved. Given that lead ammunition has been used by hunters in the condor's range for much of the last two hundred years, lead poisoning almost certainly caused many condor deaths historically.

Adult condors have few natural predators and, prior to the arrival of humans in their world, likely had a high survival rate. Animals with high adult survivorship are typically long-lived, have low reproductive rates, and invest a great deal of parental care in their offspring. One breeding attempt may take well over a year, and a pair of condors that nests successfully typically raises only one nestling every other year.

[2] *Carl G. Thelander and Margo Crabtree (eds.),* Life on the Edge: A Guide to California's Endangered Natural Resources: Wildlife *(Santa Cruz, Calif.: BioSystems Books, 1994).*

Their naturally low reproductive rate made it impossible for condors to bounce back when their numbers were decimated by shootings and indirect poisonings. Egg collecting, which was rampant in the late 1800s and early 1900s, also may have had an impact on condor populations. Egg collecting reached its peak at the turn of the twentieth century and, according to one estimate, more than seventy condor eggs had been taken by the 1940s. Although egg collecting by both hobbyists and scientists diminished by the mid-1900s, condors still could not reproduce and mature quickly enough to survive the ongoing direct and indirect human persecution.

Conservation Battles and the "End" of Wild Condors

Early condor researchers, unaware of the pervasive threat of lead poisoning, deemed habitat loss, human disturbance, and direct persecution as the principal reasons for the condor's decline. They felt that if habitat could be preserved so that condors could nest and roost without being subjected to shooting and molestation, condor numbers would increase. Such sentiments were disputed from the 1940s onward, but with no clear evidence of why condors were disappearing, habitat preservation seemed to be the most logical solution to the increasingly severe depletion of the condor's numbers. Accordingly, the Sespe Condor Sanctuary was created in California's Los Padres National Forest in 1947 to protect significant

Adult condors have few natural predators and, prior to the arrival of humans in their world, likely had a high survival rate.

condor nesting and roosting areas. Through the 1950s and 1960s, officials undertook additional conservation measures, such as increased education and law-enforcement efforts to reduce shooting and disturbance at nesting and roosting areas; additional study of the effect of poisons on surrogate species; and an end to killing coyotes by baiting them with poisoned carcasses. Nevertheless, even these measures failed to bolster condor numbers. In 1967 the California condor was declared endangered under the Endangered Species Preservation Act of 1966, a precursor to the 1973 Endangered Species Act.

A California Condor Recovery Team formed in 1973 and produced a "California Condor Recovery Plan," the first recovery plan for an endangered species, in 1975. By the mid-1970s, it became increasingly clear that traditional methods of condor conservation, namely habitat preservation and species protection, were not having the desired effect. Fewer than sixty condors existed by this time. Biologists and others recommended a more aggressive approach: the development of a captive-breeding program that would ultimately supplement the wild population, and the use of radiotelemetry (capturing wild birds and affixing radio transmitters to their wings) for tracking birds to learn more about their foraging movements, critical habitat, and mortality factors.

As condor numbers declined, political divisiveness over how to save the species reached a crescendo. The polarization of attitudes regarding what was best for condors appears, in large part, to have been the result of different perceptions regarding the species' wildness. Pioneering studies by Carl Koford in the 1940s and earlier studies by William Finley at the beginning of the twentieth century indicated that condors were relatively approachable birds that could tolerate significant levels of disturbance. During the battles to establish the Sespe Condor Sanctuary, however, the condor gained the reputation of being highly sensitive to any kind of human disturbance. It is still debated whether this perception was created, as some believe, to facilitate the establishment of a sanctuary for condors, or whether it was the result of new interpretations of Koford's data. According to Noel Snyder, former California Condor Recovery Team member and co-author of *The California Condor: A Saga of Natural History and Conservation* (2000), the early alliances to establish protected areas for the condor and the information promulgated by Koford and his allies contributed to the condor becoming "enshrined as a species too sensitive to even approach safely, too sensitive to study closely, too delicately balanced above extinction [for captive breeding to be initiated] without endangering the population."[3]

Despite these widespread sentiments, the California Condor Recovery Team called for the initiation of a captive-breeding program in 1976, a suggestion that was supported two years later by a panel of ornithological experts and the National Audubon Society. In early 1980, amidst dire prognostications from many environmental groups (including the Sierra Club, Friends of the Earth, and several local chapters of the Audubon Society) that insisted the condor be allowed to "die with dignity," free of radio transmitters and harassment by scientists, biologists took steps to initiate a captive-breeding program and to fit wild birds with radio transmitters for scientific study.

In June 1980, however, the fledgling program came to a sudden halt. In one of the earliest attempts to enter a nest to obtain baseline measurements on and information about a condor chick, researchers underestimated the seriousness of stress to nestlings and apparently mishandled both the bird and the situation. The chick began exhibiting severe stress symptoms shortly after the biologists began their work and died minutes later. The shocking death of this half-grown condor chick reverberated throughout the scientific community, as well as among conservationists, agencies, and concerned citizens. The incident further fueled the sentiment that the species was "untouchable." Permits were withdrawn and all intensive research and conservation activities stopped. According to Mike Wallace, condor expert and current leader of the California Condor Recovery Team,

---

3 *Noel F. R. Snyder and Helen Snyder, "Biology and Conservation of the California Condor,"* Current Ornithology 6 *(1989): 223.*

"the death of that chick not only brought the whole program to a complete halt, but it also came close to ensuring the extinction of the condor since it prevented the initiation of the captive-breeding program until it was almost too late."

Nearly two years later, as condor numbers continued to decline, pressure to create a captive-breeding program again increased. One of the factors leading to the resumption of plans for captive breeding was a large-scale photo-census effort developed by Noel Snyder and others in 1982. Each wild condor was photographed and identified by recognizable differences in their feather molt pattern. One bird might be recognized because it was missing an outer flight feather; another might be identified because it had lost a particular tail feather. The photo-census led to the first conclusive population count to date. Shockingly, only twenty-one condors remained in the wild. One additional bird—Topa Topa, at the Los Angeles Zoo—was in captivity, giving a total population of twenty-two condors.

In 1982 researchers finally gained permission from the California Fish and Game Commission to take eggs from wild condor pairs and restart the captive-breeding program. Researchers collected the first eggs in 1983. From the beginning, the hope was to raise condors in captivity to supplement the wild population through reintroductions. Within a few years the breeding program was well underway. Sadly, things did not progress as smoothly in the wild.

During the winter of 1984–1985, six of the remaining fifteen wild condors disappeared and were

From the beginning, the hope was to raise condors in captivity to supplement the wild population through reintroductions.

presumed dead. Tragically, four of these birds were members of breeding pairs, leaving only one intact pair in the wild. Top geneticists and condor biologists recommended bringing the last nine birds into captivity to save the species and maximize the genetic diversity of the newly established captive flock. The California Fish and Game Commission concurred, but the U.S. Fish and Wildlife Service (USFWS) agreed only to allow the capture of three of the remaining condors. These captures took place during the summer of 1985. The following December, AC-3 (for Adult Condor 3, following the original "naming" system used for condors), a wild condor that biologists had captured to replace a failed radio transmitter, showed high levels of lead in her blood. Thereafter, USFWS changed its position and supported the decision to recapture all remaining wild condors.

Within weeks, the National Audubon Society filed a lawsuit to prevent this drastic measure, alleging that the USFWS's decision was "arbitrary and capricious." Apparently Audubon felt that not only would habitat needed for future condor releases be lost if all condors were brought into captivity, but also that birds needed to be left in the wild to serve as future guides for captive-raised birds released to the wild. Until the lawsuit could be resolved,

Condor Genetics

Upon hearing that only twenty-two California condors once remained in existence, questions about inbreeding quickly spring to many people's minds. Every condor flying free today is descended from fourteen wild founders, some of which may have been related. With such a small starting population, maximizing the genetic diversity that remained in the population was imperative to minimize the negative consequences that often arise from inbreeding. When a captive population was initially established, however, the relatedness of many of the wild condors was unknown. Pairings between known parents and siblings was avoided, but little else could be done to maintain the genetic diversity of the population. Fortunately, though, the California Condor Recovery Program benefited early on from newly developed genetic techniques. In the early 1990s, the twenty-eight condors that were alive as of January 1, 1989, and four deceased condors underwent DNA fingerprinting and subsequent statistical modeling to analyze their relatedness.

Interestingly, the genetic analysis revealed that these condors could be divided into three subgroups or clans. The relatedness *between* the clans was significantly less than the relatedness of condors *within* each clan. Formerly, condors comprising the different clans and their relatives had used distinct, although overlapping, sections of the species' remaining range in southern California. Upon discovering that the extant condors consisted of these three subpopulations, biologists tried to pair birds from different clans so as to maximize the genetic diversity left in the entire population. They also sought to maximize the number of offspring produced by each of the founders.

Knowing the condor population's genealogy (and maintaining an ongoing record of it in the California Condor Studbook) has ensured that condors released to the wild are as genetically diverse as possible, that founder birds are represented genetically both in captivity and in the wild, and that birds carrying unique genes are protected by not releasing them to the wild.

Despite the care taken by an exceptional team of geneticists to maximize the diversity that existed in the remnant population, extant California condors appear to be more inbred than their Andean condor counterparts, which maintain far healthier population levels. Fortunately, California condors have not had low fertility rates or low survival rates of eggs and nestlings, two hallmarks of inbred species. Nevertheless, several embryos have exhibited chondrodystrophy (a lethal form of abnormal limb development) and have failed to hatch. Captive condors that are carriers of this recessive gene are no longer paired. It remains to be seen the extent to which such inbreeding issues will affect reproduction in the wild. For the time being, both captive and wild condor populations appear to have maintained sufficient genetic variation to reproduce and thrive.

Several of the older condors now flying free in Arizona and Utah are the offspring of the last wild condors, which were taken into captivity in California in the 1980s. Condor 122 (left) is AC-9's son, while Condor 119 (right) is AC-2's daughter.

Biologists in California attempt to capture two of the last remaining condors in the wild, AC-2 (left) and his mate AC-3 (right), luring them into the trapping area with a calf carcass on November 18, 1982. AC-3 died of lead poisoning in January 1986, possibly after ingesting lead bullet fragments found in an animal carcass. AC-2 was brought into captivity in December 1986 and spent many years raising young condors for reintroduction to the wild.

biologists suspended efforts to capture the last of the wild condors.

Meanwhile, in early 1986, AC-3 succumbed to the lead that had been found in her blood the previous December. Despite round-the-clock care and intensive treatment by dedicated veterinarians and keepers at the San Diego Zoo, AC-3 died on January 18. Condor biologist Jan Hamber had watched AC-3 and her mate AC-2 for eleven years. Two decades later, the loss still reflects in her eyes as she looks heartbreakingly at the taxidermy mount of AC-3 on display at the Santa Barbara Museum of Natural History.

After AC-3's death, only one female and four male condors remained in the wild. AC-8, the last female, selected the youngest of the males, AC-9, which had just reached adulthood, as her future mate. In early spring, the pair produced an egg that was taken into captivity. That year, biologists captured two more condors for the breeding program.

Finally, the Audubon Society lost its lawsuit on appeal, and USFWS researchers received permission to capture all of the remaining wild condors. AC-2 was captured on December 13, 1986, leaving two condors in the wild.

The move to capture the last wild condors tore the conservation community apart and incensed many who believed that condors either would not survive in zoos or would lead compromised lives, producing zoo-bred progeny that would never make it as "real" condors in the wild. Activists and protesters stalked the Los Angeles Zoo threatening to break in and liberate the birds.

Meanwhile, renowned raptor and condor trapper Pete Bloom focused on doing what he believed to be the right thing for the species and captured AC-5 on February 27, 1987. As he placed AC-5 in a kennel to be transported to the zoo, he looked up to see the silhouette of AC-9, the last condor remaining in the wild, watching him from a perch in a large oak tree.

In the weeks following AC-5's capture, AC-9 roamed southern California alone, searching for food and perhaps others of his kind. Finally, on April 18, condor biologist Jan Hamber spotted AC-9 near a calf carcass on a remote ranch north of Los Angeles. Torn between her desire to do what was required and her fear of condemning the last of the wild condors to the uncertainty of captivity, she agonized about calling Bloom to inform him of AC-9's location. Finally, though, she drove to a gas station and telephoned Bloom.

Well before daybreak on the morning of April 19, Easter Sunday, Bloom and his team hiked to the vicinity of the tree where AC-9 had roosted. He laid out a calf carcass as bait and set up a cannon net. After laying a folded net attached to several projectiles on the ground, he inserted the projectiles into small, cylindrical "cannons." At the right moment, Bloom would fire the cannons from his observation blind and the projectiles would launch out over their target, dragging the net in an arc along with them. Cannon nets had been used to catch groups of vultures in Africa, and Bloom had used them successfully on condors in California.

Anxiously, the capture team waited as the sun rose. Ravens and a golden eagle landed and fed at the carcass. Finally, just before 10:00 AM, AC-9 spread his giant wings and glided down to the carcass. As he began to feed, Bloom fired the cannons, flinging the mesh over the majestic bird. Someone gave a victorious shout. Hamber turned to them and asked, "How can you be happy about this?" Seconds later, Bloom retrieved AC-9 from the net and, with a feeling of intense sadness, folded the wings of the last wild condor. With a lump in her throat, Hamber looked at AC-9 and said, "I'm sorry."

A short time later, biologists loaded AC-9 into a large dog kennel and put him on a plane bound for the San Diego Zoo, circumventing the angry activists who were waiting at the Los Angeles Zoo for the arrival of what they perceived to be the last member of a doomed species. The capture of AC-9 represented a terrifying gamble. For some, it marked the end of a legendary creature's reign over the skies. For others, it was a flicker of light from which a phoenix was sure to rise.

A year later, the first California condor to be conceived in captivity hatched at the San Diego Wild Animal Park.

Biologists carefully extricate AC-9, the last wild condor, from their trapping net on April 19, 1987. The capture of AC-9 sharply divided conservationists, many of whom believed the move would lead to the species' extinction.

3 CAPTIVITY AND REINTRODUCTIONS

In February 1982, Jack Ingram, a nest-watcher for the U.S. Fish and Wildlife Service (USFWS), hunkered in a discrete observation blind on a remote hillside outside the Sespe Condor Sanctuary. From the blind, Ingram watched in frustration as the male member of a California condor pair repeatedly drove his mate away from their egg, a maladaptive behavior the male condor had been exhibiting for weeks. Only when hungry or thirsty did he cede caring for the egg to his eager but frustrated mate. Two years earlier, the pair (known as the CC pair) had raised a nestling without incident that would become the last wild condor, AC-9. However, this time nothing seemed to be going right.

A captive California condor peers through its extended flight feathers. The visual acuity of condors is six to eight times that of humans. The center of their field of vision is slightly magnified, allowing them to identify food at extraordinary distances.

Finally, on the morning of February 26, the determined female managed to push her way into the nest cave and, using her bill, drag the egg out from under her domineering mate. To Ingram's horror, however, the egg rolled down the slanted floor of the cave and out onto the nest cave's entrance patio. With fewer than twenty-five California condors left in the wild, the value of this egg could not be overstated. Fortunately, an unseen ledge stopped the egg from falling over the edge of the cliff. But the reprieve was to be short-lived. The condors' activities and the exposed egg had piqued the curiosity of a pair of ravens, who flew in close to investigate. Although she had quickly settled down to incubate the egg in its new location, the female was soon forced to stand up again as one of the bold ravens invaded her nest space, intent on getting itself a meal. Leaving her egg exposed, the female lunged at the intruder, attempting to drive it from her nest

Biologists had suspected for years that condors might be able to **lay a second egg** if their first one was destroyed, something observed in many other bird species, including Andean condors.

cave. Seeing his opportunity to regain control of his prized egg, the condor male in turn lunged at the female and in the chaos that ensued, the egg tumbled out of the cave and over the cliff. The priceless egg, containing a world of hope for the survival of a species, shattered on the rocks below. At the time, a despairing Jack Ingram could not possibly have guessed that this seemingly disastrous incident would be an instrumental turning point in the recovery of the California condor.

Double-Clutching Unveiled

Biologists had suspected for years that condors might be able to lay a second egg if their first one was destroyed, something observed in many other bird species, including Andean condors. Despite some circumstantial evidence, however, such suspicions had never been confirmed. With wild California condor numbers plummeting and reproduction in the wild down to an average of two nestlings per year, the California Fish and Game Commission was loath to allow the collection of wild condor eggs to initiate a captive-breeding program. Many still believed that condors were so sensitive to human disturbance that even watching their nests could lead to reproductive failure.

Disheartened by the loss of the CC pair's egg but refusing to give up their vigilance, the USFWS's condor nest-watch team continued to monitor the pair's behavior. Soon, the pair resumed pre-laying courtship activities, including investigating possible nest sites. And then, forty days after their first egg shattered, the female laid a replacement egg in a spacious cave the pair had used successfully two years before. The CC pair had provided definitive proof that condors can lay a second egg if their first is destroyed. This crucial finding, coupled with the 1982 photo-censuses that showed that only twenty-two condors remained in existence, paved the way for the issuance of permits to allow biologists to take eggs from wild condors to hatch in captivity.

Double-clutching, or the removal of the first egg to promote the laying of a second egg, became the cornerstone of the captive-breeding program and the key mechanism for reversing the steady decline in condor numbers. Removing a wild pair's first egg and raising it in captivity, thereby encouraging the birds to lay a second egg, which they were left to incubate, doubled the reproduction rate of the remaining condors. While an average of only two nestlings had been raised per year in 1980, 1981, and 1982, condors produced six young in 1983, the first year that biologists took eggs into captivity from the wild, and seven in 1984.

Remarkably, when the first egg was taken into captivity in 1983, the pair re-laid as expected, but their second egg was depredated by a raven. A month later, however, the condor pair laid a *third* replacement egg, proving that, if forced, condors were capable of *triple*-clutching. In the ensuing years, biologists in the captive-breeding program routinely pulled the first two eggs laid by each con-

Double-clutching, or the removal of the first egg to promote the laying of a second egg, became the cornerstone *of the captive-breeding program and the key mechanism for reversing the steady decline in condor numbers.*

dor pair, thereby encouraging the birds to produce three eggs per year. After declining for centuries, condor numbers finally began inching upward as a result of such manipulations. By 1987, when biologists captured the last wild condor and brought him into captivity, the condor population had increased from its low of twenty-two in 1982 to a total of twenty-seven.

Early Captive-Breeding Efforts

In 1983, however, when the first egg taken from the wild was brought by helicopter to the anxiously awaiting staff at the San Diego Zoo, no one could predict with certainty that the captive-breeding program would reverse the condor's path toward extinction. Diligent zookeepers quickly embraced their roles as vulture parents, playing tape recordings of vulture sounds, as well as moving and tapping the egg, as a condor parent would do. On March 30, a little more than a month after the arrival of the first wild condor egg at the zoo, a tiny little celebrity emerged from the egg with the help

Taking the place of a condor parent, a zookeeper at the San Diego Wild Animal Park helps a hatchling condor out of its egg. Condor chicks typically take three days to break out of their shell.

of Avian Propagation Specialist Cynthia Kuehler, who carefully extricated the hatchling. The handful of pink skin and fluffy white down was soon dubbed Sisquoc, after the Sisquoc Condor Sanctuary in Santa Barbara County, California, which had been put aside for the protection of his species in 1937. (In the early years of the program, captive-reared condors were given Native American names in addition to their studbook number.) Moments after emerging from his shell, the first California condor hatched in captivity delighted his caretakers by looking around alertly and responding to his surrogate parent, a condor hand puppet.

From the beginning, zookeepers charged with raising condors in captivity knew it would be critical to prevent nestling condors from imprinting on their human caretakers if the birds were ever to be released to the wild. As a result, Sisquoc and future baby condors were fed using a condor puppet constructed to look like the head and neck of an adult condor. Tucked behind a dark screen, a zookeeper wearing the condor puppet like a sleeve would extend his or her arm through an opening in the screen and transfer meat from the puppet's bill to the hungry nestling. Keepers also used the condor puppet to preen and interact with the chick.

During the first years of the captive-breeding program, zookeepers raised all condor eggs taken from the wild because no captive adult birds were available. As biologists brought wild birds into the captive-breeding program, however, the scientists allowed pairs of condors to raise nestlings. The zoo staff took the pair's first and, sometimes, second egg and raised them to help boost the pair's total output; the condor pair then raised the last of their progeny to gain valuable parenting skills. When young captive-raised pairs finally began breeding, their first egg was taken by zookeepers and replaced by a dummy egg until the keepers could be sure the young birds would incubate their egg appropriately. Just before their real egg should have hatched, the dummy egg was switched with the soon-to-hatch egg of an Andean condor. Given the rarity of California condors, zookeepers did not allow an inexperienced pair to attempt to raise one of their own offspring. Once a pair had proven themselves successful, capable parents, keepers allowed them to raise their own chick.

Although zookeepers successfully hatched eggs taken from the wild at the Zoological Society of San Diego (the San Diego Zoo and the San Diego Wild Animal Park) and the Los Angeles Zoo from 1983 onward, it was not until 1988 that Molloko, the first California condor conceived by captive parents, hatched in captivity at the San Diego Wild Animal Park. In the following years, captive production grew, as more and more captive condors came of breeding age. Four chicks hatched in 1989, then eight in 1990, and twelve in 1991. By the end of 1992, ten years after the initiation of the captive-breeding program and the low point of twenty-two extant condors, the California condor population had reached sixty-three birds. As space to house the condors became more limited, an additional captive-breeding site, based at the Peregrine Fund's World Center for Birds of Prey

(WCBP) in Boise, Idaho, was created. The WCBP developed and produced its first captive chick in 1996. Later, the Oregon Zoo in Portland also joined the captive-breeding effort, producing its first chick in 2004.

A Test Run with Andean Condors

Flush with the early successes of the captive-breeding program, zookeepers and the condor recovery team began initial planning for the first reintroductions of condors to the wild. At first, the recovery program sought to begin releases as soon as any wild pair had five progeny in the captive flock. Thanks to double- and triple-clutching, this goal was met surprisingly soon. By mid-1984, two wild pairs each had five captive offspring—all taken into captivity, either as eggs or nestlings. The recovery program planned to release these pairs' future offspring.

However, unforeseen events stymied the next step forward. Neither of the wild pairs whose captive-raised progeny were scheduled for release survived to the 1985 breeding season. The death of these adults, coupled with the death of two additional condors during the winter of 1984–1985, put a hold on any proposed reintroductions.

Three years of trial releases with Andean condors in southern California helped pave the way for the first reintroduction of California condors to the wild in 1992. Eventually, the Andean condors were captured and re-released in their native Colombia and Venezuela.

Despite such setbacks, the USFWS and California Condor Recovery Team continued to lay the groundwork for future releases by conducting trial reintroductions of Andean condors. In addition to helping refine future reintroduction and monitoring techniques for California condors, the experimental release of Andeans in the Sespe Condor Sanctuary, beginning in 1988, allowed the condor recovery program to test criteria used to select release sites, identify environmental hazards in release areas, and train condor biologists.

Scientists released the first three Andean condors (all females) at the Hopper Mountain National Wildlife Refuge in California in August 1988. An additional release of four more female Andeans took place shortly thereafter in the nearby Sespe Condor Sanctuary. The experimental releases continued until 1991, at which time biologists recaptured all Andeans remaining in the wild in California (they were eventually reintroduced to their native Colombia and Venezuela). Although the released Andean condors had shown a high degree of attraction to human activity and human structures, only one of the Andeans died during the course of the study, providing hope that the reintroduction of California condors would meet with similar success.

Return to the Wild

In 1992, after a five-year absence in the wild, biologists were ready to release California condors back into their native habitat. Although lead, which was thought to be one of the primary threats to condors, was still prevalent in the birds' environment, it was decided that releases would go forward. As with the Andean releases, biologists fed the newly released California condors using a supplemental food source in the hopes of keeping them inside protected areas and preventing them from feeding on carcasses containing lead.

A large group of supporters assembled on January 14, 1992, to welcome the first two captive-raised California condors back to their rightful place in the wild. The two condors, Xewe (pronounced GAY-wee) and Chocuyens (cho-KOY-yens), would be accompanied on their first flight by two Andean condors. Biologists held the Andeans with Xewe and Chocuyens in the release pen on the Arundell Cliffs in the Sespe Condor Sanctuary, with the intention of creating a larger social group for the inexperienced youngsters. The night before the release, USFWS biologists removed the netting on the release pen; the condors would be free to fly as soon as they felt inclined on Release Day the following morning.

As it turned out, *neither* felt inclined to fly the following day. Instead, the young birds explored the sandstone edge of the release cliff, flapping and hopping about but not taking flight. Their cautious return to the wild mattered little to the excited onlookers encamped on a distant cliff, who celebrated the momentous day nonetheless, choked with emotion while imbibing champagne.

The following day, Xewe spread her wings and took to the skies. The recovery team could not have asked for a more appropriate and auspicious beginning to the reintroduction program. When biologists removed AC-9 from the wild amidst heated debate, no one could have guessed that fewer than five years later, AC-9's captive-raised daughter, Xewe, would be the first to take his place flying free over California.

Despite the elation that greeted the return of condors to the wild, the reintroductions in California proceeded far from smoothly. Only seven months after her release, Xewe was shot at while perched on a boulder on U.S. Forest Service land near Pyramid Lake. Two men on a family outing decided to try out a new .22 caliber rifle on the temptingly large, black-feathered target. Amazingly, the bullet missed Xewe, as did a second that the men fired at the fleeing bird. Unbeknownst to the men, a USFWS technician was watching Xewe at the time of the shooting, and one of the men eventually received a $1,500 fine and three years probation for the incident.

Xewe escaped with her life, but Chocuyens was not so fortunate. On October 8, 1992, Chocuyens was found dead near Pyramid Lake, after having ingested ethylene glycol from an unknown source. In December 1992, six additional condors joined Xewe in the wild, but between the following May and October, three of these died from either colliding with or being electrocuted by power lines. A fourth died the same way in June of 1994. The birds also showed a disturbing attraction to human activity and human structures. Birds that were overly curious about people, had a tendency to land on houses, or regularly perched on power poles were eventually returned to captivity.[4]

Determined to give the condors every chance at success, Mike Wallace, a leading expert on vulture reintroductions and head of the California Condor Recovery Team, initiated aversive conditioning as a means of better preparing condors for the challenges inherent in the ancient bird's modern habitat.

"At first people were pretty skeptical about the idea," Wallace recalls. "I was told at one meeting that my idea of subjecting the condors to a mock power pole that would be electrified so as to give the birds landing on it an electric shock would never work." But Wallace and his colleagues persisted. The USFWS constructed another release pen in a more remote site at Lion Canyon in the Los Padres National Forest, and equipped this, as well as all future release pens, with an electrified mock power pole.

The power poles were a remarkable success. What had been the greatest source of fatalities for reintroduced condors became a negligible source of mortality in the ensuing years. With such innovations, the number of condors in the wild inched upward.

---

4 *Xewe was among those condors returned to captivity in 1994. She now serves as a highly successful mentor bird for juvenile condors in the pre-release pen at the reintroduction site in Baja, Mexico.*

Currently, biologists are reintroducing California condors in California, Arizona, and Baja California. Each release site is administered by a different entity and is supported by a diverse array of cooperators. In Arizona, condors are released to the wild by the Peregrine Fund (TPF), which was founded in 1970 by Tom Cade to address the plight of the peregrine falcon. TPF developed captive-rearing and release methods for peregrines and helped supplement the falcons' dwindling numbers in the wild by reintroducing hundreds of captive-raised birds. In 1984 TPF's captive-breeding facilities were consolidated and moved to Boise, Idaho, becoming the World Center for Birds of Prey. TPF later expanded its mission to working to conserve birds of prey in nature nationally and internationally.

Based largely on its successes with raising and reintroducing peregrine falcons and, later, species such as the Mauritius kestrel (*Falco punctatus*) and the Aplomado falcon (*Falco femoralis*), to the wild, the Peregrine Fund was contracted by the USFWS to have their World Center for Birds of Prey serve as a captive-breeding facility for California condors, and for TPF to conduct the releases and subsequent monitoring of condors in Arizona. Since 1996, the majority of the day-to-day work in the field with condors has been conducted by TPF, and most of the condors currently flying in Arizona have been raised at the World Center for Birds of Prey.

TPF is supported in its efforts in Arizona by the National Park Service, Arizona Game and Fish Department (both of which have condor biologists who have made vital contributions to the program over the years), USFWS, Bureau of Land Management, U.S. Forest Service, Utah Division of Wildlife, and others. While TPF receives support from the USFWS for their efforts, more than half of its yearly budget for condors comes from donations by foundations and individuals committed to helping restore the California condor.

In addition, several other groups support the condor program. In the past, Grand Canyon National Park's condor biologist was funded entirely by the Grand Canyon National Park Foundation, a nonprofit organization dedicated to protecting the canyon's natural, cultural, and historical resources. Condor education efforts undertaken by the National Park Service Division of Interpretation in the park have received substantial funding from the Grand Canyon Association, a nonprofit group that supports education, research, and visitor services at the canyon.

Several organizations and government agencies have contributed to the reintroduction program in northern Arizona. A soaring condor over the vastness of the Grand Canyon is now a common sight at Grand Canyon's South Rim.

Finding a Home-Base for Condors in Arizona

With releases in California underway, the California Condor Recovery Team and its cooperators began planning another vital component of the Recovery Plan. Keenly aware of the vulnerability of small populations of animals, the recovery team sought to ensure that condors would survive as a species even if they contracted an unknown disease or were decimated by a natural calamity. Their plan recommended the establishment of three distinct populations of California condors: a captive population, a California population, and a third population in an area geographically separate from the California population within the condors' historic range. But where should a third population be established?

As early as 1981, the San Diego Natural History Museum's prescient Curator of Birds and Mammals, Amadeo Rea, recommended the Grand Canyon region as the best place to reestablish the beleaguered condor. While other naturalists were debating whether or not a captive-breeding program should be initiated, Rea was already thinking about *where* captive-bred condors should be reintroduced. The choice, for him, came down to one of the four areas where condors remained when Europeans began settling the West: the Pacific Northwest, the Grand Canyon region, northwestern Baja California, and south-central California. Interestingly, Rea felt that the *worst* choice would be to reintroduce the birds to California, where

the last condors before implementation of the captive-breeding program seemed unable to survive, much less thrive. The best choice, he was convinced, was the Grand Canyon region, which seemed to have everything a condor could ever need.

"This is prime habitat," Rea wrote in his 1981 Recovery Proposal for the species, "rugged terrain with open areas and strong updrafts. . . . The Inner Gorge of the canyon is a massive expanse that is self-contained with relatively limited human intrusion. Because this is a national park, firearms are completely prohibited. Throughout the canyon are caves, many of them undoubtedly traditional nesting sites . . . [that] are completely safe from molestation. . . . [In addition] there is a readily available source of megafauna in the canyon."

Although the Grand Canyon seemed like a perfect place for condors in theory, to a practical biologist like Mike Wallace, the region posed as many potential problems as benefits for reintroducing condors. The remoteness that made Grand Canyon an ideal place for condors also made it a challenging place for field biologists to follow and monitor the vulnerable, newly released birds.

"Although it sounded great in theory, I just couldn't see how to make the Grand Canyon work," Wallace recalls. "Then one day, I was up in a plane, flying high over northern Arizona and I saw the perfect set of cliffs—the perfect place for releasing condors." Back on the ground, Wallace pored over maps trying to figure out which cliffs he had seen from the air.

"I finally found what I'd been looking for—the Vermilion Cliffs." A massif of vibrantly colored, sheer red sandstone, the Vermilion Cliffs ring the Paria Plateau, which juts out of the earth north of Grand Canyon National Park. "The site had everything: high exposed cliffs to keep condors safe, winds to give them lift, isolation from people and development, and ready access for field crews to care for and monitor the birds pre- and post-release."

After numerous visits to the area by those involved with condor recovery in Arizona, a release site was selected atop the cliffs on the Paria Plateau in the Vermilion Cliffs Wilderness area, today part of Vermilion Cliffs National Monument. Draft reintroduction plans, public comment periods, and highly contentious public meetings followed.

Ultimately, the proposed releases in Arizona were facilitated by the decision to release condors there as a "10j" species. Section 10(j) of the Endangered Species Act allows the USFWS to classify federally listed species that are to be released to the wild as "nonessential experimental" populations. To be designated as such, a nonessential experimental population must be reintroduced outside the species' current range, but within its historical range; its release must further the conservation of the species; and its existence must not be considered essential to the continued survival of the species. Wolves reintroduced into Yellowstone National Park are perhaps the best known "nonessential experimental" or "10j" species.

Such a designation ensures that current land uses and activities, such as agriculture, mining, livestock

grazing, sport hunting, and recreation, will not be restricted. On USFWS and National Park Service lands, however, a nonessential experimental population is treated as a threatened (though not endangered) species. A threatened species does not automatically have protection under the Endangered Species Act; an endangered species automatically gains certain protections.

The 10j boundary for the condors to be reintroduced at the Vermilion Cliffs incorporated southern Utah, western Nevada, and northern Arizona. Within this boundary, landowners could continue all legal activities even if condors were present on their land.

At first the 10j designation and the proposed 10j boundary caused some confusion among the public. Area residents objected to the government subjecting them to an "endangered" species and all the regulations that they believed would come along with such a species on their land. At the first public comment meeting in Kanab, Utah, hostile area residents shot a barrage of furious and bitter comments at attendant meeting facilitators and federal officials. Ultimately, though, patient and persistent USFWS biologists managed to reassure at least a portion of the skeptical crowd that the presence of condors would not threaten their livelihoods.

Nevertheless, in the spring of 1996, Utah's San Juan County filed a lawsuit to stop the reintroductions. The court case stalled the first proposed release of nine condors in Arizona, which had been scheduled for that June. Ultimately, the lawsuit was unsuccessful and, after years of effort by a dedicated group of cooperators (represented by the USFWS, Arizona Game and Fish Department, National Park Service, Bureau of Land Management, U.S. Forest Service, Peregrine Fund, Hualapai Indian Tribe, Navajo Nation, Los Angeles Zoo, Zoological Society of San Diego, Phoenix Zoo, and California Condor Recovery Team), the release of the first captive-raised condors in Arizona was set for December 1996.

All reintroductions in Arizona were to be conducted by the Peregrine Fund, a nonprofit group specializing in the reintroduction of endangered birds of prey. Largely based on the group's successes with rearing and reintroducing endangered peregrine falcons throughout the United States, the USFWS contracted them to carry out the releases and subsequent monitoring of condors in Arizona.

The Return of the California Condor to Arizona

Over a frenetic twelve days in October 1996, a Peregrine Fund field crew built a forty-by-thirty-foot (12-by-9-m) release pen atop the orange sand and rock at the rim of the Vermilion Cliffs. On October 29, one condor raised at the Peregrine Fund's World Center for Birds of Prey and five condors raised at the Los Angeles Zoo were flown to Page, Arizona, where they were greeted by reporters, photographers, and an excited group of project cooperators. The condors were then transferred to the release site in a helicopter.

The six youngsters, Condors 133, 136, 142, 149, 150, and 151, adjusted quickly to their new home, feeding eagerly on the stillborn calf carcasses that the field crew snuck into their enclosure under the cover of darkness, and coping well with frigid temperatures and successive snowstorms.

On the morning of December 12, 1996, car after car trundled up the dusty gravel road that runs through the House Rock Valley below the western end of the Paria Plateau and the towering Vermilion Cliffs. Soon hundreds of photographers, reporters, dignitaries, and condor aficionados had assembled to watch the condors' historic first flight. Bundled against the cold, Secretary of the Interior Bruce Babbitt told a joyful crowd that the impending release will "bring this landscape full cycle." He compared the reintroduction of condors in Arizona to the return of wolves to Yellowstone and praised the use of the Endangered Species Act for such environmental restoration. Then, he led the crowd in a countdown: "Five, four, three, two, one. . . ."

An excited crowd of about one thousand people gathered below the Vermilion Cliffs on December 12, 1996, to watch condors flying free in Arizona for the first time in over seventy years.

As nightfall fell, silence and solitude once again enveloped the Vermilion Cliffs. ∽

High up on the Vermilion Cliffs, Mark Vekasy, field manager for the Peregrine Fund's Condor Reintroduction Program, stealthily opened the door to the condors' pen, being careful not to alert the condors to his presence. A lean, intense man of quiet words who is passionate about large birds, Vekasy felt a nervous excitement course through him as he played his historic part in opening the condor's way to Arizona's azure skies. Tentatively, the six condors emerged from their enclosure and extended their giant wings, feeling the wind rush under their feathers. As the crowd assembled far below roared in delight, Condor 150 stepped into the wind and was suddenly airborne. For Vekasy, though, there was only deep silence as the bright sunlight danced over the rocks and sand, followed by the symphonic sounds of the wind whistling through condor wings as the first of his charges embraced her freedom.

Keeping Condors Flying

As nightfall fell, silence and solitude once again enveloped the Vermilion Cliffs. The cars had left, the dignitaries and journalists had returned home, and the field crew was left to begin the unrelenting and often unglamorous work of watching over and caring for Arizona's first group of wild condors. Each day the field crew assembled at the release area. One or two of them carried out their duties "up top," as they dubbed the release site atop the Vermilion Cliffs. After traveling northward along the House Rock Valley, they drove up the Paria Plateau through a gap in the cliffs. After nearly an hour on a four-wheel-drive-only road of deep sand and unforgiving ruts and rocks, they bumped and heaved along the top of the plateau until reaching a sandy parking area. After depositing their camping gear in a canvas tent, they walked through deep sand to a cramped blind that overlooked the release pen and the condor feeding area. From the dark confines of the blind, the biologists could watch the condors feed and drink and soar over their cliff-top home.

Every few nights, a biologist on up-top duty donned a bulky garbage can attached to a stiff backpack frame and carried calf carcasses weighing as much as eighty pounds (36 kg) each along the sandy path down to the cliff edge, a headlamp weakly lighting the way in a landscape of rock pinnacles. After placing the carcasses along the rim while condors slept on the cliffs below, the biologist returned to the shelter of the tent, heated up a quick meal, and then laid down for a few hours of sleep on a stiff cot. Just after daybreak, the condor caretaker hiked back down the sandy trail and ensconced himself or herself in the small blind that provided such a magnificent view over the condors' world.

Meanwhile, back down in House Rock Valley, additional crewmembers settled in for a long day of looking up at the Vermilion Cliffs through powerful spotting scopes (a telescope designed for watching wildlife) and binoculars from beneath a rustic lean-to shelter. Dubbed "the Ramada," the shelter provided the only shade for miles around. From their vantage point, they could watch the birds as they lounged on the cliff face, out of view for the biologists on top of the cliffs. The biologists in the valley began each day at the Ramada by cycling through all the condors' radio-transmitter frequencies to ensure that each bird was present.

Having determined the rough location of each bird based on the direction of the signal being emitted by its radio transmitters, the biologists then made a visual search for each condor with their spotting scopes. The scopes allowed the field crew to read the tag numbers on each bird's wings despite being about a mile away from the cliffs. The crew could also mobilize at a minute's notice and head after a condor that had decided to expand the

Reintroduced California condors gather around a calf carcass at the Vermilion Cliffs release site in northern Arizona. A hungry group of condors can reduce a calf carcass to a skeleton in under an hour.

boundaries of its known world. On such an occasion, the biologist listening to a particular bird's radio frequency heard that the signal was moving. Even if they could not spot the bird flying high above the cliffs, perhaps obscured by clouds, they could follow the progress of its transmitter signal using their receiver and directional antenna (known as a Yagi). They then jumped in a truck and drove down whatever roads they could find to stay close to the bird and monitor its progress. If it landed in an unsafe spot, such as the valley floor, they hiked in and "hazed" (flushed or chased) the bird to a safe perch, thereby keeping it safe from predators until it

In May 1997, when warm weather finally settled on the Vermilion Cliffs and small purple flowers blanketed the House Rock Valley, the Peregrine Fund released nine additional condors to the wild.

learned the survival skills that its parents would ordinarily have taught it. Within a few months after the first release, the field crew was doing more driving and tracking than sitting and watching.

Despite the crew's dedication, however, they were powerless to protect the young condors from all threats. After not being able to visually locate Condor 142 for several days and noting that the bird's radio signal remained stationary in the direction of a little cove just south of the release site, the

crew hiked in and, to their dismay, found the condor's body near the base of the Vermilion Cliffs. Killed by a puncture wound to the head inflicted by an eagle's talons, Condor 142 had survived less than a month in the wild. His death was a sobering reminder of the many challenges the field crew and their young charges would face in the future.

In May 1997, when warm weather finally settled on the Vermilion Cliffs and small purple flowers blanketed the House Rock Valley, the Peregrine Fund released nine additional condors to the wild. Reintroduced as a group of four on May 14 and a group of five on May 29, these condors comprised the birds that had been slated for release in June 1996, prior to the filing of the injunction by Utah's San Juan County. Concerned that the original group that was slated for release was now too old, the condor recovery program opted to hold back the nine birds hatched in the spring of 1995 in favor of a December 1996 release of the condors hatched in the spring of 1996. After the encouraging behavior of the 1996 birds, however, biologists decided to go ahead and release the 1995 birds, hoping that the benefits of having fellow condors in the wild would outweigh the unknown risks of releasing birds that had spent their first two years of life in captivity.

By mid-May, fourteen condors soared over the Vermilion Cliffs, the two-year-olds quickly adapting to their life in the wild and mimicking the one-year-olds' newfound skills at flying, roosting on the cliff face, and finding food. Sadly, Condor 151, who had been part of the first release in December 1996, struck a power line and died near Page, Arizona, on May 18; she is the only condor in Arizona to date that has perished in this way. The condors' numbers were further diminished by the loss of Condor 128, which disappeared in July, only two months after being released to the wild. Despite these difficult losses, the Peregrine Fund crew persisted with their efforts to track and watch over the condors. In November 1997 they released another four birds to the wild.

On the Long Road to Recovery

As 1997 drew to a close, fifteen young condors flew over Arizona, while another twenty-four flew wild in California and an amazing ninety-three comprised the captive population. A decade after the last wild condor was pulled from the skies and taken to its new zoo home, the condor population numbered 132 birds.

Not only were condor numbers steadily growing in Arizona during the first year of reintroductions, but their range was expanding rapidly as the birds flew increasingly farther afield. After several months in the wild, the birds had traveled over an area with a radius of about one hundred miles (160 km) from the release area. Five of the condors, Condors 116, 119, 128, 133, and 136, delighted visitors when they showed up at Utah's Bryce Canyon National Park in June 1997, traveling first to Kayenta, Arizona, west of Monument Valley Tribal Park (a flight of approximately ninety miles [145 km]), then over to Bryce (a distance of approximately 120 miles [193 km]). To the field crew's

relief, the condors flew the fifty miles (80 km) back to the release site after spending just a few days in Bryce.

Less than a month later, on July 6, 1997, the Peregrine Fund field crew received a report of a condor sighting in Moab, Utah, some 180 miles (290 km) north of the release site. Condor 149 had been missing for several days when she was spotted by a former condor biologist from California who must have been amazed by the sight of a young condor being harassed by a pair of golden eagles over Moab's colorful cliffs.

This flight was later eclipsed by those of ever more wide-ranging condors. On July 31, 1998, Condor 119, which had been released to the wild as a two-year old in May 1996, disappeared from the release area. Unrelenting in his quest to find his missing charge, Shawn Farry, who had succeeded Vekasy as field manager, made an aerial search over a several-hundred-square-mile area and drove countless miles over northern Arizona and southern Utah looking for the errant bird. After several days, he finally heard the satisfying blips emitting from his receiver, which indicated that the wandering condor, which was still 110 miles (175 km) from the release site, was heading back to the Vermilion Cliffs. The following week, when they received a report from a Boy Scout troop that had seen the bird, the field crew realized how epic 119's journey had been: Condor 119 had made a six-hundred-mile (966-km) round-trip flight to Flaming Gorge National Recreation Area in the southeast corner of Wyoming.

Although no condors released in Arizona are known to have surpassed 119's flight to Wyoming, others have made truly impressive journeys. Condors 116, 122, and 123 flew to Grand Junction, Colorado, in June 1999. Condors 176 and 191 flew to Mesa Verde National Park, Colorado, less than a week later. And in March 2004, Condor 246 logged an impressive 550 miles (885 km) as he virtually circumnavigated northern Arizona, traveling first from the Vermilion Cliffs to the Sedona area, then heading westward to the vicinity of Show Low (near the New Mexico border), and finally returning to the South Rim of the Grand Canyon via Flagstaff.

Journeys such as Condor 246's would have gone undetected in the past unless a reliable report confirmed his presence in a particular area. However, the use of satellite transmitters (a device that uses satellites to triangulate the bird's position and then transmits the information via satellite to a computer where it can be downloaded by biologists) on a few of the Arizona condors beginning in August 2001 greatly facilitated the mapping of condor travel. Over time, the increasing use of such technology will provide much more information about the wanderings and explorations of these adventurous, wide-ranging creatures.

Radio Transmitters and the Science of Tracking Condors

Each condor released in Arizona wears two radio transmitters (either one on each wing or one on a wing and one on the tail). Condors wear different transmitters than large raptors, such as eagles and hawks. Raptors are usually outfitted with "backpack" transmitters, which attach to the bird's back with straps that go under and over each wing and meet at the bird's chest. Condors, however, feed by filling their expandable crop with large quantities of meat. Because their chest area expands to accommodate their swelling crops, condors cannot wear backpack transmitters because the straps would hinder crop expansion. Instead, current California Condor Recovery Team leader Mike Wallace and his colleagues developed patagial transmitters that condors can carry on their wings. Each transmitter weighs 2.1 ounces (60 g) and represents about 0.6 percent of the bird's body weight. A small hole is pierced (equivalent to human ear piercing) through the condor's patagium, a thin membrane of skin that forms the leading edge of each wing. The post that anchors the transmitter is put through the patagial hole, and the stud is held in place with a tiny locking nut that screws onto the post. The small transmitter rides comfortably on top of the condor's numbered wing tag, its antenna pointing backward toward the condor's tail.

Biologists tracking condors carry a receiver that detects the radio waves broadcast by each condor's transmitter. Each transmitter has a different frequency. The biologist can dial in a particular bird's frequency, then follow the bird's signal and, therefore, its movements, using a directional antenna (known as a "Yagi") that plugs into the receiver. Biologists can also set their receivers to scan through all the condor transmitter frequencies to determine which condors are in the vicinity.

Biologists working with condors in Arizona have received transmitter signals from condors as far as seventy miles (112 km) away. To receive a bird's signal from such distances, the bird needs to be flying high above the ground, and the biologist needs to be on a high point unobstructed by hills or cliffs. Because radio signals are blocked by cliff walls, when a condor drops into a canyon, its transmitter may have a range of only a mile or so.

Although solar-powered radio transmitters have been used with mixed success in the past, most condors in Arizona, California, and Baja California carry conventional transmitters that contain a small nickel-cadmium battery. These batteries typically last about a year, at which time the condor must be recaptured and outfitted with a new transmitter. Each year, one of the major tasks facing the field crews overseeing condors is to recapture the entire condor flock to replace their transmitters.

The author searches for condors near Navajo Bridge, in the northeastern corner of Grand Canyon National Park, using standard radio-tracking equipment: a hand-held receiver and a "Yagi" antenna. By checking for signals on the unique frequency of each reintroduced condor's radio transmitter, biologists can determine which condors are in the vicinity and approximately where each bird is located.

Increasingly, conventional transmitters are now being exchanged for solar-powered satellite transmitters. These transmitters, which are similar in shape and weight to the conventional transmitters, beam their signals up to receiving satellites. The satellites then send data down to a receiving computer that transmits the bird's coordinates to a biologist's computer. Satellite transmitters have revealed exciting data about the daily movements and peregrinations of condors. However, there is a lag of about twenty-four hours between when a transmitter sends a signal and when a biologist receives the bird's coordinates on his or her computer. As a result, birds carrying satellite transmitters also carry conventional transmitters, so that, if a condor gets into trouble, a field biologist can quickly track it.

Monsoon clouds blanketed the Grand Canyon, while the rains that they had so recently spawned drew out a vibrant palette of colors from the jumble of cliffs and buttes below me. Forced to yell so that the new field crewmember, Paul Flournoy, could hear me over the gusts of wind, I pointed into an area known as The Abyss. "Based on their radio-transmitter signals, I'd say there are nine condors down there," I shouted. "With that many birds clustered together in one area, I expect they've either found a carcass or a really fun toy."

In a landscape where cliffs are often more abundant than trees, California condors reintroduced to the Southwest take advantage of the abundant rocky ledges for roosting and resting. Condors use the many caves that pockmark the cliffs in canyon country as nest sites.

Flournoy glanced at me in surprise, but made no comment as we lifted our binoculars to our eyes and began scanning the cliffs and talus slope far below us. Seconds later, I laughed and Flournoy stared in astonishment at the veritable condor play-fest that met our eyes. The winds had blown a garbage can lid and several pieces of trash over the rim. While dismayed, as always, that trash had found its way into the canyon, I could do little but sit back and enjoy the show.

A small, empty water bottle hurtled into the air, launched by a condor's bill, then tumbled down-slope, our dominant condor in hot pursuit. Jumping over a small bush, six-year-old Condor 123 ran down the bottle and then propelled it into the air again. Several condors gave half-hearted pursuit and then stopped to watch 123 chase his prize before searching out toys of their own. Condor 127 soon found another water bottle and began chasing it around,

Such **bouts of play** are quite common for condors and likely have adaptive value.

jumping into the air and flapping her wings in mock surprise whenever her bill sent the bottle flying into the air.

Condor 114, meanwhile, entertained himself by chasing a tin can until a more exciting object suddenly caught his sharp eye: the garbage can lid!

Realizing that 114 had discovered a higher form of entertainment, Condors 119 and 127 abandoned their toys and rushed over to join him. Condor 114, a superior dragger-of-large-objects (I once watched him pull a large plywood board around for hours), grabbed the lid in his bill and tried to drag it. But he was foiled by Condors 119 and 127, who seemed to find it far more entertaining to stand *on* the lid, walking along its perimeter and biting its edges while 114 tugged on it. Reluctant to leave such diversions, the condors continued playing until well after their usual roost time. A few tired of these antics a little earlier than the rest and resorted to another of their favorite games—King of the Bush—wherein the birds battle and push each other to capture the choice spot standing atop a particular bush. As darkness closed in, the condors finally turned their backs on the entertainment and, one by one, flapped laboriously up to the safety of the cliff to roost for the night.

Condor Play and Dominance Hierarchies

Such bouts of play are quite common for condors and likely have adaptive value. While at first glance two condors playing tug of war with a stick or a condor dragging around a wooden board seems to have little survival value for the birds involved, seeing the same condors tugging at a hide to tear open a carcass or battling over a piece of meat suddenly puts their play in perspective. Play is thought to contribute to motor and sensory development. The strength, speed, agility, confidence, and aggression that condors develop while playing may help them compete more successfully at carcasses as they grow older. Nevertheless, some of the play behavior exhibited by condors may have no better explanation than pure enjoyment or the dispersal of excess energy, and may be similar to the seemingly purposeless play we see in other intelligent creatures. Ravens, for example, have been observed climbing up snowy hills and sliding back down on their backs, behavior which seems to have no other explanation than sheer entertainment for the creatures involved.

In addition to their playfulness, California condors, like other scavengers such as ravens and turkey vultures, are exceptionally curious, intelligent, and opportunistic. Condors are also social creatures that typically fly together, feed together, roost together, and even bathe together. For most of us, such interactions are more likely to bring to mind a pack of puppies or a troupe of monkeys than a group of carrion-feeding birds.

Condors also have a highly developed dominance hierarchy; younger birds are submissive to older birds, and, within a cohort or age group, males are generally dominant over females. This hierarchy is developed during squabbles at carcasses, fights over choice roost spots, aerial tail chases, and,

Three-year-old male Condor 187 (right) exerts his dominance by claiming a perch from two-year-old female Condor 210 (left). Averting his face to avoid 210's lunging bill, 187 will push forward until he forces the younger bird off the ledge.

more subtly, through neck-wrestling bouts. During these bouts, young condors will either stand or lie together and repeatedly entwine necks, while pushing at each other with their chests. Invariably, the more submissive bird is pushed off the ledge or perch on which the two birds are wrestling. Over time, these neck-wrestling bouts and the success a particular bird has had at getting food at carcasses or claiming perches help determine where the condor stands in the dominance hierarchy.

Once a bird's dominance is established, it often needs to do little to assert itself. When a dominant male lands at a carcass, submissive birds immediately back away. The behavioral cues that a dominant or submissive bird may transmit to others are further emphasized by the bird's plumage. The contrasting black-and-white plumage and vibrant head coloration of adult condors are a marked contrast to the mottled underwing and black heads of the juveniles, and the coloring likely highlights an older bird's status.

California condors are exceptionally curious, playful, and intelligent. They often key into the activities of other scavengers, like this common raven, to help them find food.

When a condor lands on a rock outcrop next to another condor, it is often clear which is the dominant bird. Unlike challenges between wolves or gorillas, in which the dominant animal stares down a subordinate individual, which in turn shows its deference by averting its gaze, a dominant condor will approach a lesser-ranked individual with its neck turned and its face averted. This posture allows the dominant condor to avoid the inevitable pecks thrust its way by the subordinate condor. Ignoring the lunging bill of the submissive condor, a dominant condor will continue its forward momentum and, face averted, push the subordinate condor off its preferred perch.

Condor Intelligence

Condor intelligence has not been measured scientifically. While their intelligence may not match that of the common raven, whose high intelligence is widely acknowledged by researchers and whose scavenging habits condors closely mimic, condors seem capable of problem-solving in a manner that resembles raven behavior. Zoologist and renowned raven expert Bernd Heinrich of the University of Vermont has tested raven intelligence by hanging pieces of meat at the end of strings attached to perches. The ravens exhibited cognitive intelligence by using insight and a multiple-step thought process to attain their goal of getting the suspended meat. The ravens pulled up on the string to draw

the meat closer, then held the string in place with a foot, and then again pulled up on the string. This process was repeated five or six times until the meat was within reach.

Kris Lightner, a former field biologist for the Peregrine Fund, once observed Condor 127 engage in a similarly insightful, multiple-step thought process. Watching from high on a cliff rim overlooking Badger Beach in the Marble Canyon portion of Grand Canyon, Lightner observed Condor 127 propelling an empty water bottle along the beach with her bill. As the bottle arched away from her, Condor 127 gave chase until it was within reach; she then sent it airborne again. But, as she shuttled the bottle along the shoreline, she inadvertently moved it closer and closer to the water's edge. Suddenly, a small wave lapped at the bottle and pulled it out into the river, where the current whisked it downstream. In vain, 127 ran down the beach watching and keeping pace with the bobbing water bottle.

Moments after the bottle seemed lost, the river swept it into an eddy several feet from the riverbank. Condor 127, intent on retrieving her toy, waded out in the water and stretched her neck toward the bottle, but she could not quite reach it. Looking around, she spied a partially submerged boulder bulging out of the water and hopped onto it. Stretching out her neck again, she was now able to reach the bottle and nudge it toward the riverbank. As it drifted toward the beach, Condor 127 hopped off her boulder into the water and gave the bottle another push toward shore. Soon, she and the water bottle reached the beach, and 127 resumed her frenzied play, propelling and then chasing the bottle along the beach.

"I know it's anthropomorphizing," Lightner said, referring to the attribution of human emotions or characteristics to an animal, "but 127 seemed crushed when she lost her bottle and she seemed so excited when she was able to retrieve it and could play with it again." Clearly, this behavior showed a degree of intelligence—a step-by-step thought process—rather than rote, trial-and-error learning.

Condors feeding at large carcasses are exposed to a complex social environment in which they interact with other avian and mammalian scavengers, as well as potential predators. The need for scavengers to evaluate their situation and make a variety of adaptive decisions that will allow them to feed safely, compete with other scavengers, and avoid predators every time they encounter a new carcass likely explains why much of scavenger behavior appears to be learned rather than innate. Their need to function successfully in their complex environments may also explain why scavenging birds quickly learn new tasks, and why they are considered to be among the most intelligent birds.

Condors and Humans

For those who have worked with condors, the playfulness and intelligence of the species are only parts of their appeal. As important, perhaps, is that each individual condor has a readily identifiable personality. Every condor in existence today is accounted for, and all but the few that hatched before the founding of the recovery program have been monitored and observed for their entire lifetimes. Each bird that hatches in captivity is known intimately by the captive-breeding staff who have watched over it. This knowledge is passed on to the field crews who are responsible for each bird's welfare once it is reintroduced to the wild. Through direct observations, field notes, and stories that are passed on from one successive field crew to the next, each condor's history is documented, talked about, and speculated upon.

As much as we delight in each condor's unique personality and history, and in the intelligence and playfulness universally exhibited by the species, the birds' inherent curiosity and lack of wariness toward humans can lead them into trouble in our rapidly developing world. As one of the largest avian members of the scavenger feeding guild (a group of species that exploits a common resource base in a similar way) for thousands of years, condors likely had few natural enemies. Although they seem to have developed an innate fear of canids (members of the wolf and coyote family) and felids (members of the cat family), their wariness of humans appears to be far less developed. In a book written by biologists Helen Snyder and former California Condor Recovery Team member Noel Snyder, the two discount the claims of a few early researchers that the historic wild condors were extremely wary, stating:

Wild condors have continued to have a contrary habit of flying in curiously from a distance to circle low over hikers' heads, sitting placidly for frame-filling portraits by wilderness photographers, accepting banana peels and peanut butter sandwiches from back-country explorers, and walking unconcernedly along the shores of a heavily-boated lake with waterskiers whizzing along only a few meters away (all are documented occurrences).[5]

The Snyders elaborate on the tameness exhibited by the wild condors that existed prior to the reintroduction program by citing several of their own close encounters with these birds. One condor pair walked within fifteen feet (5 m) of them along a lakeshore even though they were in full view. Another flew low over their heads and landed near the top of a fir tree only a few yards away. Paying them virtually no attention, the condor yawned, preened, and rested, even as they moved in for a closer view.

Although some early researchers claimed condors were wary creatures, their own data and those of other researchers belie these claims. One famous photograph from 1906 shows William Finley, one of the earliest condor biologists, with his hand on the back of a wild nestling condor while the parent condor looks on from a distance of only a few feet. Finley and a photographer climbed up to that particular condor's nest, removed the nestling, and photographed it throughout the nestling period while the parents curiously looked on.

"While we were getting pictures of [the nestling]," Finley later wrote, "the parents sat . . . only a few feet away. They were almost devoid of fear, for several times they stood within five or six feet of us in perfect unconcern."[6]

Despite their relative tameness, condors from the historic wild population were not known to come voluntarily into settled areas. Whether this was because of an aversion to human development, a lack of such development in the condor's historic range, or a combination of these things is not known. Furthermore, not all condors were equally unwary. While certain condors nesting near settled areas seemed undisturbed by and tolerant of human presence and activities, condors in more remote areas appear to have been less approachable. Wild condors also appeared to be wary of humans in certain vulnerable situations, such as when feeding on a carcass.

---

5 *Noel F. R. Snyder and Helen Snyder,* The California Condor: A Saga of Natural History and Conservation *(San Diego: Academic Press, 2000), 69.*

6 *William L. Finley, "Life History of the California Condor, Part III: Home Life of the Condors,"* Condor *10, no. 2 (1908): 65.*

Although wild condors seem veritably tame compared to birds such as golden eagles, some of the juvenile condors reintroduced in the first years of the recovery program showed an unprecedented lack of wariness toward humans, an excessive curiosity about human activities and structures, and a proclivity for putting themselves into dangerous situations.

The absence of parental guidance likely contributed to this lack of wariness. Juveniles of many species seem to be more confiding toward humans than do adults. Without the presence of condor parents to serve as behavioral examples, reintroduced juvenile condors are more likely to endanger themselves.

Some of the first juvenile condors released in California did indeed put themselves in dangerous situations. In perhaps the best example, several birds landed on roofs in the small community of Pine Mountain Club, adjacent to Los Padres National Forest in Kern County, California. Aside from tearing at roof tiles and ripping at screen doors, several of the birds entered a building by dropping into an open skylight. While this event was highly publicized and seized on by critics who felt that the reintroduced condors could never behave as their wild ancestors had, the possible reasons behind this behavior received little media attention. Either excited by the prospect of seeing condors up close or, as at least one U.S. Fish and Wildlife Service (USFWS) biologist has alleged, to prove that the reintroduction effort was a failure because of continued bitterness about the capture of the original wild condors, several members of the community enticed condors into the area and onto their homes by placing hotdogs along their porch railings. Once given a food reward, the juvenile condors were understandably loath to give up their newfound play area, and they had to be recaptured and returned to captivity. Early release cohorts in Arizona and central California also contained problem birds that approached people, landed on buildings, showed no concern for their own safety, and had to be recaptured.

Teaching Condors to Be Wild

In response to such behavioral problems, researchers continually refined rearing techniques to reduce habituation of nestling condors to humans and to better mimic the behavior of parent condors toward their nestlings in both captive and wild situations. They also made several changes in the management of juvenile condors pre- and post-release.

Field crews seeking to improve the behavior of newly released condors in the wild took a multi-pronged approach that recognized the importance of adult mentors, the different rates at which young condors develop socially, and the use of aversion training, brief "time-outs," and prolonged detention as tools for modifying condor behavior.

Realizing the importance of having juveniles interact with experienced adult birds, the California release sites placed an adult mentor bird in prerelease pens with the juveniles awaiting reintroduction. While the Arizona release site did not adopt this method, the proximity of free-flying older condors ensured that the Arizona juvenile condors would interact with older birds.

In addition to benefiting from the presence of mentors prior to gaining their freedom, with each successive release, juvenile condors increasingly had older birds accompanying them in the wild. The improvement in the behavior of these juvenile condors was apparent when comparing the behavior of the first released cohorts with subsequent release groups. The benefit of introducing young condors into an existing population was further brought home in Arizona with the initiation of a second release area.

In November 1998, a cohort of juvenile condors was released for the first time at a new site on the Hurricane Cliffs, about seventy miles (115 km) west of the Vermilion Cliffs release site and twenty-five miles (40 km) south of St. George, Utah. A second release group followed in November 1999. Interestingly, individuals in these cohorts showed far more behavioral problems than birds that had recently been released at the Vermilion Cliffs. Not having older birds as examples, the Hurricane birds seemed to have a greater proclivity for approaching humans.

The 1999 cohort was particularly problematic. After one juvenile died from aspiration while feeding on a carcass and another was killed by an eagle, the five remaining condors left the release area to explore their surroundings. One disappeared and was never seen again. Over a period of a few days, three out of the four remaining Hurricane condors were recaptured after landing and approaching people in northern Arizona (one at Pipe Springs National Monument,

Juveniles of many species seem to be more **confiding toward humans** than do adults.

one in a mobile home park in Fredonia, and one on a farm in Cane Beds).

With the return of these three birds to captivity, the field crew decided that the Hurricane Cliffs release site was not as desirable as the one on the Vermilion Cliffs, because of the difficulties the condors released there had in the wild and because of the difficulty its location presented for management of the releases. Because the Arizona flock used the Vermilion Cliffs as a home base, juvenile birds released at that site now had older birds whose behavior they could mimic, unlike birds released at the Hurricane Cliffs. After two releases at the Hurricane Cliffs in 1998 and 1999, all future condors in Arizona were released to the wild at the Vermilion Cliffs. Birds from these later releases exhibited far fewer behavioral problems than did the ill-fated Hurricane Cliffs birds.[7]

In addition to benefiting from the presence of older birds, juvenile condors released at the Vermilion Cliffs benefited from other refinements in release strategies initiated in 2001. Having determined that young condors develop socially at different rates, the Arizona field team decided to release birds when they

---

[7] *After spending time in captivity, all recaptured Hurricane Cliffs birds were ultimately re-released to the wild from the Vermilion Cliffs release site.*

California condors in Arizona are typically recaptured at the Vermilion Cliffs release site. A large mesh pen similar to a dog kennel is baited at night with a calf carcass. A door into the pen is held open with a cable that leads to a nearby observation blind. A biologist hides herself in the blind in the darkness preceding dawn and awaits the arrival of the birds. Soon after first light, the condors suddenly appear, soaring at high speeds over the cliffs against the dramatic backdrop of the morning sky. Unaware of the onlooker hidden in the blind, the condors land on or near the enclosure and stare at the carcass. When the condors are finally hungry enough to overcome their nervousness about the strange wire restricting their access to the food, they locate the door and tentatively walk into the trap. The biologist quickly pulls the cable, shutting the door and enclosing the condors.

Not surprisingly, over time, condors become increasingly wary of the trap and are less inclined to enter, even for a juicy calf carcass. I have spent hours in agonized frustration as a particular bird loafed near the trap but refused to go in, or went in only to run out again before I could close the door. Fortunately, the release area has another irresistible draw to facilitate trapping: juvenile condors. While the adults become increasingly wary of the trap, newly released condors are always in the area. These naïve birds have not yet developed a fear of the trap, and they are all too eager to get to a meal that the adults seem to be ignoring. Adult condors, upon seeing the juveniles gorging in seeming safety on the carcass, find it difficult to resist taking over a feeding opportunity from subordinate condors. Running into the trap, they seek to displace the youngsters, grab a quick bite, and rush out again. While these wary older birds are more difficult to catch, patience and the hunger of young condors usually make it possible.

From 2004 onward, the Peregrine Fund increasingly used the pen in which condors are released to the wild as the condor trap. Because of its much larger size, the pen could accommodate more condors at a carcass, allowing many more condors to be trapped at one time. Once a group of condors enters through the large gate at the front of the pen and starts feeding, a biologist hidden in a wooden compartment at the back of the pen turns a winch to lower the entrance gate and trap the birds.

Once condors are trapped, biologists enter the pen holding an enormous fishing net. One biologist carefully drops the net over one of the condors (no easy feat in an enclosure holding numerous panicked birds with nine-foot wingspans). A second biologist quickly moves to restrain the condor's head, removes the netting, and tucks the condor up under his or her arm. Condors will bite viciously when they feel threatened. Therefore, when handling condors, a primary goal is to

immobilize the condor's head. In addition, handlers try to keep its powerful wings folded, and to restrain the condor's strong legs and feet, preventing the condor from pushing against the handler to get free. Accordingly, when drawing blood or replacing transmitters, three people typically hold a condor while a fourth does the needed work. The condor is gently placed on someone's lap.

That person holds the body and keeps the wings tightly folded. A second person holds the head, and a third holds the legs. Once the work is finished, the biologists carry the condor to the cliff's edge or to the top of a slight incline and then gently lower the bird to the ground. Within seconds the condor beats its powerful wings and launches itself back into the safety of the sky.

Superbly adapted for soaring flight, California condors are wide ranging and may spend many hours a day flying. Several times a year, biologists recapture every free-flying condor to replace their radio transmitters and to test the birds' blood for the presence of lead.

Over time, the hazed condor will opt for natural perches and maintain a safer distance from humans. ∽

were deemed "ready" to be released, as opposed to releasing an entire cohort of juveniles on a given date, as had been done previously. In March of 2001, only five of the eleven birds awaiting reintroduction in the flight pen were selected for release, while the remaining six were left in the pen for some additional "growing-up" time. The field crew selected the condors to release based on their dominance status within the flock, their behavior toward people, and their weight. (In the past, heavier juveniles had shown less of a tendency to get into trouble with people than lighter ones, and heavier birds were less likely to become dangerously underweight while learning to compete successfully with adult condors for food.) In the ensuing months, with the most dominant youngsters no longer present in the flight pen, submissive birds stepped up to become the dominant members of their flock, competing more successfully at carcasses and growing warier of people as more months passed in isolation from humans.

Initially, such a release strategy was met with some resistance, because multiple small releases per year as opposed to one publicized release "event" received less media attention (several release sites are administered by nonprofit groups dependant on donations generated through publicity). The higher survivorship and improved behavior of birds that were "trickled" out

rather than being released as a single large group, however, made a convincing case for multiple small releases, and release sites in central California and Arizona ultimately adopted this strategy.

After the release of juvenile condors, field biologists continue to modify condor behavior through a variety of hazing techniques, used every time a young condor approaches humans or human structures. Over time, the hazed condor will opt for natural perches and maintain a safer distance from humans. Because condors are gregarious and curious, a naïve condor landing on a building will often entice older condors to land nearby and investigate. As a result, it has been critical to haze juveniles every time they transgress, so the entire flock does not descend to the lowest common denominator demonstrated by an overly tame youngster.

For the field crew that is responsible for modifying the behavior of an irrepressibly curious and fearless juvenile condor, the task can sometimes seem hopeless and daunting. Kris Lightner, a former field biologist for the Peregrine Fund, certainly felt an overwhelming sense of frustration and helplessness on a crisp fall day in 2001 when she chased young Condor 210 (affectionately known as "two-ten") all over the North Rim, hoping to convince her to leave the area. Held back an extra year because of her antisocial behavior toward other condors and lack of wariness around people, Condor 210 was released as a two-year-old in December 2000. After remaining near the release area for months, 210 headed for the developed area of the North Rim in September 2001.

Much to our dismay, 210 touched down near one of Grand Canyon National Park's housing areas adjacent to the busy command-and-control center for firefighting operations on the North Rim. As Lightner chased 210, trying to haze her from this very unsuitable place, 210 fled through the surrounding forest on foot and via short flights. Probably confused but fascinated by the activity and chaos in the area, 210 refused to leave, instead making repeated short hops from one bad spot to another. Several firefighters tried to corner the miscreant condor, but 210, which could easily have qualified for a Condor Olympics sprinting event, eluded them and led Lightner on a breathless chase through the forested housing area. At one point she hopped up onto the windowsill of a maintenance building. Running inside, Lightner grabbed a broom from a stunned maintenance worker and, thrusting it through the open window, pushed 210 off the ledge.

As 210 rushed to take cover and Lightner raced

Condor 210 flares her wings as she lands on a pinnacle at Grand Canyon's South Rim. Overly curious and tame as a juvenile, 210 was taught to be more wary by biologists who repeatedly chased her away whenever she landed too close to humans or human structures.

to catch up to her, something caught this inexperienced young condor's eye and stopped her dead in her tracks. A *toy*! A small, bright-orange ball lay on the ground, and 210 paused to push it around with her bill. But the relentless biologist soon closed the gap, forcing 210 to abandon her newfound toy and flee. Shortly afterward, 210 took off in earnest and landed high up in a ponderosa pine on the outskirts of the North Rim Campground. In relative safety, she finally settled down for the night, and Lightner returned to the field house.

With heavy hearts, Lightner and I headed back to the North Rim well before dawn the following morning, capture-net in hand. We planned to recapture 210 if she showed any inclination to repeat the prior day's antics and to subsequently hold her in captivity for a while to give her more growing-up time. A few hours after sunrise, 210 left the safety of her perch and flew in the direction of the camp-

A few hours after sunrise, 210 left the safety of her perch and flew in the direction of the campground.

ground. Attracted by the activity of several ravens on the ground next to the campground, 210 dropped down to join them. Unwilling to allow her to perch on the ground even in a nearly empty campground, Lightner and I raced toward her. The moment she saw us headed her way, 210 started to

run and, a few seconds later, took off, landing high up in a ponderosa on the rim of the canyon. Unlike the day before when she had moved from one bad spot to another, 210 had moved from a bad place to a good one upon being hazed. Perhaps the previous day's harassment had not been completely in vain. Not long afterward, she caught a nice updraft and, soaring high into the sky, left the North Rim and headed back to the safety of the release site.

Despite the hints of progress Condor 210 had made at the North Rim, her behavior seemed little improved when she arrived for the first time at Grand Canyon Village on the South Rim the following spring. Catching the field crew by surprise, she arrived without our knowledge and proceeded to exhibit the most abysmal possible behavior: landing near people and even grabbing at one person's shoelaces with her bill. Fortunately, 210's unsupervised behavior was short-lived. Over the ensuing days, the park's condor biologist, Chad Olson, and the Peregrine Fund field crewmembers doggedly followed her, chasing her off whenever she landed near people. Slowly, 210's behavior improved. Whereas we had had to haze her multiple times a day for her first few days at the South Rim, within a week, days passed without any need to haze her at all. By the following year, Condor 210 had become a model condor, keeping her distance from people and perching on safe South Rim rock pinnacles and cliff ledges. As an adult, Condor 210 now spends most of her time in the more remote areas of the Grand Canyon and the Kaibab Plateau, often going months without encountering people. Condor 210 proved that even the worst young condor's behavior can improve with time—and a little harassment.

For problem birds like 210, the field crew uses hazing in combination with recapture and detention time to modify behavior. Condors that show little sense of their own safety, such as landing in places that have no ready escape route, are recaptured and returned to captivity. After several additional months in captivity, the transgressor is again released to the wild. Such recapturing followed by a little growing-up time in captivity has greatly helped in reducing problem behavior.

Fortunately, such unwary young birds are the anomaly. As many as eleven condors have been released in each of the last five years in Arizona, but typically only one or two per year exhibit behavior that requires recapture. Sadly, these few individuals garner the most attention. It is far more interesting for a journalist to write about the one young condor that lands next to a person at the South Rim and tries to eat their shoelace (which probably looks like an intriguing piece of intestine to the naïve condor) than it is to write about the numerous condors that are flying free, keeping their distance from people, and feeding and reproducing as wild condors should. As a result, the bad behavior exhibited by a couple of released condors is often overemphasized in the press, resulting in a misrepresentation of the reintroduction program.

Nonetheless, condors that are raised in captivity and released to the wild are clearly capable of a dan-

Condor 210 proved that even the worst young condor's behavior can improve with time—and a little harassment.

gerous level of unwariness toward humans if their behavior is not closely monitored and modified when necessary. Under the tenure of prior field managers for the condor reintroduction program in Arizona, it has been a priority to closely monitor the movements and activities of young birds and to be on hand to haze birds the minute they put themselves into undesirable situations. As the flock in Arizona continues to grow, it remains to be seen whether such aggressive management tactics will be maintained at a high enough level to keep condors behaving like the wild condors of the past.

As I sat atop a cliff overlooking Badger Rapids, binoculars held to my face, future condor behavior was the last thing on my mind. Caught up in the moment, I laughed at the antics of the condors tearing around on the riverside beach far below me. Condor 196 raced down the beach holding the handle of a plastic one-gallon jug in her bill. Condors 227 and 198 followed in hot pursuit. Unable to see where she was going because the milk jug blocked her view, Condor 196 rammed face-first (or rather milk jug–first) into a boulder. Momentarily stunned, she sat back on her legs, regained her balance, and ran off in another direction, the other condors close behind. Eventually, Condor 227 commandeered the entertaining toy. Tossing the jug into the air, he watched it arc in the air and come back down, landing squarely on his back. Leaping in mock fright, wings jerking outward, he turned upon the opaque monster. Then, picking it up in his bill, he again tossed the milk jug skyward—and again leapt in mock fright as it landed on his back. Unnoticed by the condors playing far below me, I couldn't stop smiling as I watched them frolic on the beach.

Watching condors at Grand Canyon National Park's South Rim, visitors are likely to see perched condors suddenly extend their giant wings and keep them stretched outward for minutes at a time, as though showing off their spectacular wingspan. In fact, the condors are engaging in a behavior known as sunning. Sunning is widespread in both the New and Old World Vulture families, and it is also seen in storks, pelicans, cormorants, anhingas, and other unrelated birds. In water birds such as cormorants and anhingas, sunning appears to be a way of drying out their wings. California condors and other vultures also invariably extend their wings to the sun's rays after bathing to dry out their feathers. Nevertheless, condors also sun when their feathers are dry. Sunning is seen most often in the morning after condors wake up from their roosts. As soon as the morning light touches their bodies, the birds extend their wings to the sun.

No one is certain how this behavior benefits the birds. The two most likely hypotheses are energy conservation and feather conditioning. Many vulture species reduce their body temperatures by several degrees at night, likely as a means of conserving energy. A bout of sunning in the morning helps raise the body temperature back to normal daytime levels in preparation for their foraging flights. After long stretches of soaring, the flight feathers of large vultures can become bent from air pressure while flying. After a bird has landed, it takes several hours for a bent feather to return to its normal position, reducing the efficiency of the wing if the bird has to take off again quickly. Experiments have shown, however, that feathers warmed by the sun resume their normal shape much more quickly (because the sun heats the keratin comprising the feather shaft) than feathers

Female Condors 149 (left) and 119 (right) engage in a bout of sunning on a pinnacle below Grand Canyon Village. Vultures often "sun," either to warm their body temperature or to restore the shape of flight feathers bent from air pressure during the day's flying.

kept in the shade. This may explain why condors often sun for short periods after landing or late in the day.

On cloudy days even the faintest glimmer of sun induces a bout of sunning. On the last day of 2001, I sat bundled against the cold in a dark blind, watching the juvenile condors awaiting release in the pen atop the Vermilion Cliffs. It had been snowing off and on. As a shaft of sunlight finally pierced through the clouds in mid-afternoon, all eleven young condors simultaneously extended their gleaming wings to catch the sun's tenuous warmth. It was an extraordinary sight. At precisely the same time, down in the valley below the cliffs, field biologist Courtney Harris saw a similarly spectacular sight on the cliffs, jotting down in her field notebook, "Every condor that I see is sunning!" Moments later, having shaken off the snow and warmed themselves, at least twenty of the free-flying condors took to the skies.

5 CONDORS AT GRAND CANYON

On April 18, 1997, when Condor 136's great shadow passed over the sheer rock walls just below the North Rim for the first time, no one could have predicted the impact that she and the other members of her flock would have on visitors to Grand Canyon National Park. Nor could anyone have imagined how condors would transform an already magnificent vista into an unsurpassable, dynamic scene that would wed the timelessness of the canyon with the urgency of a modern-day fight to save an extraordinary creature from extinction. In the wild a mere four months, 136 was the best flier among the first group of condors to be released, and she was also the one most given to exploring new areas. It was not surprising to the biologists monitoring the condors that Condor 136

Reintroduced condors first discovered the Grand Canyon in April 1997, four months after they were initially released in Arizona. Since then, condors have become permanent inhabitants of the canyon, making Grand Canyon National Park's South Rim the most reliable place to see a California condor in the wild.

That the condors appreciate the winds and space the canyon offers is of little surprise to most people. ✑—

was the first to discover the Grand Canyon. Drifting along on rising thermals and breezy updrafts, Condor 136 suddenly soared out over the immensity of the canyon. The other condors were quick to follow. As they explored the canyon's vast wildness, deep silences, hidden waterfalls, and kaleidoscopic cliffs, the condors soon discovered another side of the Grand Canyon: its hordes of visitors.

Condors and Crowds

That the condors appreciate the winds and space the canyon offers is of little surprise to most people. More baffling to those unfamiliar with the species is why condors are often seen flying over the most developed areas of the park or lounging on the cliffs below Grand Canyon Village as hundreds of tourists shuffle along the rim above them.

During the Pleistocene and historic times, condors were likely attracted to large herds or congregations of animals, because it was among such gatherings that births and deaths were most likely to occur. Where animals were born, afterbirth and young animals vulnerable to predators were a readily available food source for the attendant scav-

engers. Why patrol empty landscapes when food could reliably be found where animals gathered in significant numbers? Today, the Arizona condors have a vast wilderness to fly over, but, as in years past, it is the activity and commotion of the "herds" at the South Rim that draw them. However, the herds of mammoths, camels, and ungulates that roamed the area during the Pleistocene have been replaced by vast congregations of humans today. Were it not for backcountry rangers, helicopter rescues, and emergency medical care that reduce human casualties to negligible numbers each year, condors might be right in thinking that such an aggregation would provide abundant food.

Aside from being attracted to the activity and commotion of the large human herds that patrol the canyon's rims, the condors are further drawn to these areas by the abundance of other scavengers. Condors rely on their eyesight rather than their sense of smell to find food, and they often focus on the activities of ravens and turkey vultures to find their meals. These species are present in large numbers at the North and South rims. Human handouts and easily accessible garbage attract ravens,[8] and turkey vultures have several traditional communal roosts in close proximity to Grand Canyon Village. Although condors are not interested in

---

[8] *Wildlife-proof garbage cans were installed in Grand Canyon National Park in 2004, which may help reduce the amount of human food available to ravens.*

Many of the California condors in Arizona spend day's end resting on the cliffs below Grand Canyon Village's Lookout Studio patio. Here, a fascinated public can listen to an interpretive ranger's informative condor talk while enjoying unparalleled views of the largest flying land bird in North America.

An interpretive ranger at Grand Canyon
National Park shows off a California condor
flight feather during an afternoon condor pres-
entation. These talks often coincide with the
birds' visits to the South Rim, providing tourists
with unparalleled views of condors.

eating the human garbage that the ravens seek, they never fail to investigate the activities of ravens, because these wily creatures are often the first to find the animal carcasses on which the condors depend.

Despite their interest in human crowds and their attraction to the abundant scavengers that patrol the canyon rims, it is unlikely that condors would continue to frequent the area if they were not rewarded for their efforts. Large animal carcasses, on which the condors depend for food, are abundant at the North and South rims and in the adjacent Kaibab National Forest. The condors find mule deer that have perished close to the Bright Angel Trail and other areas frequented by tourists, mules and bighorn sheep that have fallen to their deaths, and elk that have been hit by vehicles on the roads leading to and from the developed areas.

Viewing Condors at Grand Canyon

The predictable attendance of condors at Grand Canyon Village provides visitors with exceptional viewing opportunities. Indeed, Grand Canyon National Park is the easiest and most reliable place to view free-flying California condors in the world. Although many visitors now come to Grand Canyon specifically to see condors, most come to view the canyon and are unexpectedly captivated by the extraordinary sight of a bird with a nine-foot (3-m) wingspan passing overhead. Visitor after visitor has exclaimed to park rangers and condor field crewmembers that seeing condors was the highlight of their trip to Grand Canyon.

Keeping an eye on the condors at the South Rim one evening in June 2001, I was approached by a woman who tentatively asked me if I knew where condors could be seen. I pointed out two young condors that were cuddled together on a cliff ledge, and she told me, with tears in her eyes, that her father had shown her a condor in California many years earlier. Pointing to a large shape perched in a eucalyptus tree, he had told his impressionable young daughter, "That's something you'll never see again in your life." Listening to her, I couldn't help but feel how extraordinarily privileged we are that this man's prophecy failed to come true and how fortunate canyon visitors are to see wild condors soaring overhead.

Although the California condor is not unique in its status as an endangered species, the opportunity for the general public to view such a rare animal is uncommon indeed. Many endangered species are tiny and relatively unknown outside of scientific circles. Many more remain out of the public's eye in captive-breeding facilities or reintroduction sites that are closed to the public. But at Grand Canyon, tourists have opportunities to view one of the world's most spectacular endangered

CURRENT EXPERIMENTAL NON-ESSENTIAL RANGE
OF CALIFORNIA CONDORS IN THE SOUTHWEST

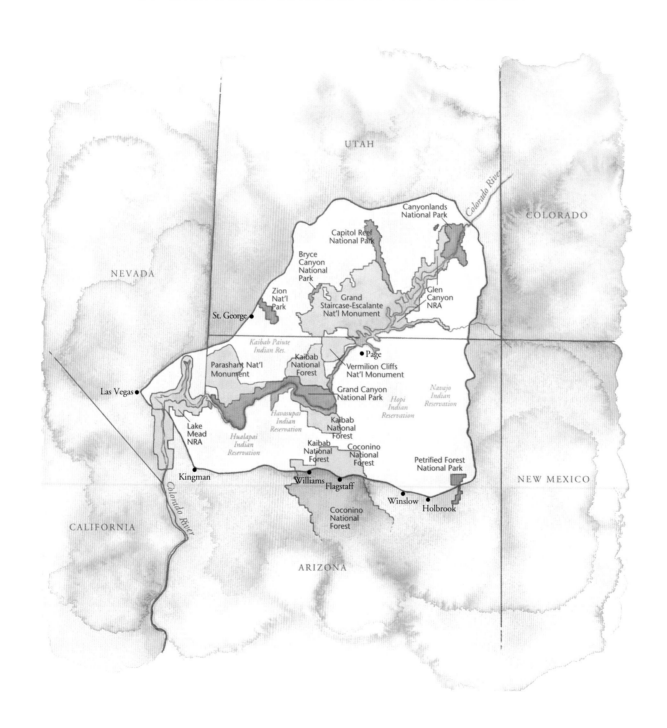

creatures and witness the unfolding of a massive reintroduction and conservation effort.

Unwitting ambassadors for the Endangered Species Act and for the conservation of other beleaguered species, the condors often seem to time their regular visits to the South Rim to thrill the many tourists who gather daily to listen to the National Park Service's summertime condor talks.

The condor talks given by the rangers have increased in popularity with each passing year. In 2004 attendance at the talks reached such high levels that the rangers started offering two talks per day on the South Rim and one talk per day on the North Rim. More than 14,000 visitors attend condor talks at Grand Canyon annually.

Condors are most easily viewed at the South Rim between March and July. While several breeding-age condors now reside in the canyon year-round, they generally venture above the rim infrequently during the fall and winter months. As the weather warms, the rest of the condor flock, which typically spends the fall and winter at the Vermilion Cliffs release site or in the Colorado River corridor, joins the older birds at the South Rim. More than thirty condors have been seen at one time on the cliffs below Grand Canyon Village in March. The opportunity to see significantly more condors than existed as a species in 1982 certainly illustrates how successful the condor reintroduction program has been. Condors also can be seen in the northernmost section of Grand Canyon National Park on the cliffs adjacent to Navajo Bridge in April and May. While condors frequent the North Rim developed area during the summer, they congregate in this area in smaller numbers, so they are seen less frequently there than they are on the South Rim.

By August, condors are seen less reliably at the South Rim as they increasingly frequent the cooler Kaibab Plateau, especially remote portions of the North Rim and the North Kaibab Ranger District of the Kaibab National Forest, and the adjacent canyons. During the fall, the availability of large animal carcasses shifts to the plateau, and the condors follow suit. Perching high in conifers on the plateau, condors are difficult to find and view during this time, although deer hunters may see a con-

Condors are most easily viewed at the South Rim between March and July.

dor land and feed at the remains of their kills. In winter, the nonbreeding birds typically spend several months loafing at the release site, making the most of the abundant food and roosting together in a relatively protected area of Vermilion Cliffs National Monument. Although the condors used to frequent the Marble Canyon area from below Glen Canyon Dam to just downstream of South

*The presence of people who do the condors no harm makes it difficult to **teach the birds that humans** are potentially dangerous and should be feared.*

Canyon between February and April, the birds seem to be spending less time in this area with each passing year, opting instead to travel to the South Rim earlier.

Condors are also being seen with increasing regularity in and around Zion National Park in southwestern Utah, particularly in the summer and fall. Many birds now spend several months there before returning to the Vermilion Cliffs release area.

Wild Condors amidst Human Civilization

While the condors' presence at the South Rim provides a unique viewing opportunity for the public, the proximity of condors and humans creates many challenges for the reintroduction program. The presence of people who do the condors no harm makes it difficult to teach the birds that humans are potentially dangerous and should be feared. It is also

difficult to teach condors to be wild in a setting where animals from squirrels to deer and ravens to coyotes approach humans and move casually in their midst. As long as condors are perched somewhere that affords an easy escape route, many show little fear of tourists and will allow their close approach. However, the condors that frequent the South Rim spend as much time outside the national park as they do in it. Outside the park boundary, they are vulnerable to being shot if they are not sufficiently wary. Although the complacency toward people that some of the condors develop at the South Rim does not teach them to stay out of rifle range, the condors do appear to be more fearful of people when outside the national park, particularly if they are perched in vulnerable locations.

For example, I have seen Condor 158 allow tourists to approach within a few feet when he was perched on the cliff edge or on a rock pinnacle at the South Rim. Yet, when I spotted him on the ground in one of the meadows on the Kaibab Plateau north of the national park, I was unable to get within two hundred feet (60 m) of him before he flushed and rapidly flew away from me.

The seeming tameness of condors inside the national park often concerns visitors, many of whom appear to hold these birds to a higher standard of behavior than they do other wildlife in Grand Canyon. Ravens walking amongst tourists' feet by the ice cream shop, coyotes begging from passing cars, and mule deer and elk strolling on the lawn around

El Tovar rarely alarm the public, but condors landing on a hiking trail or allowing people to approach them at a viewpoint typically elicit concern. Several instances of condors landing near people on a hiking trail have in fact been caused by the nearby presence of a carcass. In March 2003, for example, a pack mule fell off the South Kaibab Trail's Skeleton Point and plunged into a narrow ravine. The mule's location, its tough hide, and the cold weather that kept the carcass partly frozen for several days made it difficult for condors to eat the seemingly available food. As a result, the birds clustered together on a ledge above the carcass, waiting for an opportunity to access the tantalizing meal. Unfortunately, the ledge above the mule happened to be a section of the popular South Kaibab Trail, meaning the condors were continually approached by hikers. Unwilling to leave the food behind, the condors would periodically flush when a person approached too closely, but they would quickly return to their waiting spot to be on hand in case the meat became available. In doing so, they gave concerned tourists the impression that they were overly tame.

Hazing Condors at Grand Canyon

Despite the inherent challenges of teaching captive-raised condors to be wild in a heavily visited national park, the Peregrine Fund and National Park Service personnel have long practiced a campaign of hazing condors whenever they perch too close to humans. Since the arrival of the first release cohort to the South Rim, biologists have been on hand to teach the condors to use acceptable perches (rock pinnacles that are inaccessible to people) and behave appropriately among the hordes of tourists. Such a task can often be stressful and embarrassing for the biologist who has to harass an unwary condor in

Since the arrival of the first release cohort to the South Rim, biologists have been on hand to teach the condors to use acceptable perches (rock pinnacles that are inaccessible to people) and behave appropriately among the hordes of tourists.

front of dozens of onlookers. Although biologists try to explain their actions to viewers prior to hazing a condor, talking to every person in the area when a condor is in a dangerous or unacceptable position is not always possible. More times than I can count, I ran at unwary condors yelling or clapping to chase them away while cries of "Leave them alone, they're beautiful!" and "Stop! What are you doing?!" and "We're going to report you" reverberated in my ears. Having chased off the miscreant condors, I would explain to my critics that we were encouraging the condors to keep their distance from humans

Noisemakers have also been used to haze condors when a **bird was on an undesirable** but difficult-to-reach perch.

to keep them safe outside the park. In every case, those who had heckled me moments before were appeased and often responded with gracious thanks for the work we were doing.

Although hazing sometimes seems to have little effect on condors that stubbornly fly from one vulnerable perch to another, such consistent and persistent harassment over time has dramatically improved not only the behavior of individual condors but also the behavior of the Arizona flock as a whole. In the first few years of the reintroduction program, condors visiting the South Rim often landed on the roofs of the hotels along the rim, on railings at viewpoints, on the rock wall that lines the rim in Grand Canyon Village, and even on a lamppost adjacent to the Bright Angel Lodge. Now, with more condors than ever spending time at the South Rim, condors typically land on distant rock pinnacles in the cove below Grand Canyon Village, some distance from tourists walking the Rim Trail. Occasionally, a condor newcomer to the South Rim will land on top of Lookout Studio, a building perched on the rim that was designed to blend with the rocky cliffs below. Even though the top of

Lookout Studio is a relatively safe place for condors, Peregrine Fund and National Park Service personnel will quickly haze an inexperienced condor choosing to perch on the building, so as not to encourage other condors to land on human structures—even if they do look like part of the cliff. After being hazed, the young condor usually realizes that all the other members of its flock are landing on the cliffs below the crowds and will soon do the same.

Hazing techniques typically include running at the problem condor to chase it off. Sometimes yelling or clapping accompanies the rush toward the bird. When birds are on more inaccessible, but still undesirable, perches, biologists will sometimes get the condors' attention by clapping and then throw small handfuls of sand toward them. Perhaps because they need to be wary of rockfall in their cliffy environment, condors flush readily when they see sand or gravel falling toward them, and such a technique can increase the distance at which they will flush from an approaching human.

Noisemakers have also been used to haze condors when a bird was on an undesirable but difficult-to-reach perch. The noisemaker can sound like a firecracker or a gunshot, and the condors typically beat a hasty retreat upon hearing such a loud noise in their vicinity. Because of the noise and the concomitant spark of the noisemakers, though, they are virtually never used in the national park because firing them may alarm tourists and could spark a fire in the hot, dry summertime.

Condor 122 soars past Grand Canyon National Park's El Tovar Hotel. While juvenile condors occasionally landed on the roofs of Grand Canyon buildings in the early days of the reintroduction project, biologists used aversive conditioning to teach the condor flock to avoid human structures.

How to Help Condors at Grand Canyon

Those involved in the condor reintroduction program work hard to shape the condors' behavior at the South Rim and in other developed areas. There are a number of ways that visitors to Grand Canyon National Park can also help condors stay wild. First, refrain from feeding *any* wildlife while in the national park. When most people are approached by wildlife, their first inclination is to think that the animal must be hungry. Although many abide by the numerous signs and notices telling people not to

Ravens that are drawn to people offering food quickly attract curious condors.

feed wildlife, too many visitors do not. Dozens of animals die or have to be killed every year in the park as a direct result of having been fed by tourists. Others die as an indirect result when they are hit on the road or shot because they have become habituated to roads and people.

Feeding ravens is especially detrimental to condors because condors key in on the activities of these scavengers to find carcasses. Ravens that are drawn to people offering food quickly attract curious condors. This has been particularly problematic at Plateau Point in the Grand Canyon, where mule

riders and other tourists used to (and may still) toss their lunch leftovers to the opportunistically attendant ravens. Having watched the ravens forage successfully in this area, condors have now focused on this viewpoint and frequently patrol it in the springtime. The six-mile (10-km) one-way hike to Plateau Point from the South Rim makes it a particularly difficult area for biologists to police. Upon spotting a tourist approaching a condor at Plateau Point, biologists on the canyon rim can do little but look on in frustration: the tourist and condor would be long gone before the biologist could hike down there to haze the condor and talk to the visitor. Because condors are infrequently hazed from this inner-canyon overlook, are never harmed by people there, and are often offered food, some condors have exhibited greater levels of unwariness at Plateau Point than anywhere else in the national park. Such a lack of wariness around people puts these individuals at risk when outside Grand Canyon and makes it difficult to teach these parentless birds that humans are dangerous and unpredictable—a vital lesson if they are to survive in our modern world.

Creeping up to a condor to get the perfect photograph is a far more innocuous though no less damaging activity than feeding wildlife. Although the presence of a condor perched on a rock pinnacle at the edge of a cliff is a tempting subject for anyone with a camera, those who resist the temptation to approach the condor will help the species succeed in the long run. Most people who approach a condor to take a photograph mean no harm. Nevertheless, the seemingly innocent action of sneaking up to a bird and then backing away gives a condor the dangerous impression that humans are not a threat.

Those visitors to Grand Canyon who do not feed wildlife and who enjoy condors from a distance can relish in the fact that they are helping a magnificent creature adjust to and be successful in our rapidly changing world.

One of the greatest challenges Grand Canyon's condors face is to survive and reproduce in an area with huge numbers of visiting humans. Simply not feeding any wild animals while in the national park and surrounding natural areas is one of the best things a visitor can do to help ensure condor survival.

Condor 186 had a troubled youth. Hatched at the Los Angeles Zoo on April 15, 1998, and raised in captivity by zookeepers, Condor 186 was released to the wild in Arizona with seven other young condors on November 18, 1998. Part of the first group of condors to be released at the Hurricane Cliffs, Condor 186 interacted well with the other members of his release cohort, readily joining them at carcasses and in flights over their new home. It was not until 186 began exploring the environs of the Hurricane Cliffs that the field crewmembers watching over him had their first inklings that he was going to be an exceptional young condor—an exceptionally problematic condor, that is.

Despite incremental increases in California condor population numbers, the outlook for the species remains uncertain. Securing the condor's future likely will depend on the willingness of hunters to use nonlead ammunition within the condor's range.

On March 25, 1999, Condor 186 joined Condors 176 and 191 on one of his first major flights away from the release area. Although 191 soon returned to the safety of the Hurricane Cliffs, and 176 went on to more remote haunts, Condor 186 was attracted to the activity of an RV park near Hurricane, Utah. By the time Shawn Farry, then field manager of the condor reintroduction program in Arizona, caught up with the errant condor, it was well after dark, and 186 was roosting in a tree at the base of a cliff at the edge of town. Worried about the power lines, roads, and people in the area, Farry flushed 186 out of the tree and down to the ground at first light, and then captured him using a net gun. He returned Condor 186 to the release pen atop the Hurricane Cliffs for a time-out and then released him back to the wild on April 2.

Farry hoped that 186's recapture and time-out would teach the young condor to be more wary of people. But only days after being re-released, 186 was in trouble again. Unbeknownst to Farry and his field crew, who were feeling relieved that the young condor had headed into the seemingly safe remoteness of the Grand Canyon, Condor 186 soon came across a party of river rafters and, dropping down to river level, approached to within several feet of them. Two days later, on April 6, Farry received another call about the miscreant condor. This time, Condor 186 was at a small, remote airstrip at Grand Canyon West on the Hualapai Indian Reservation. The condor had landed on the airstrip and readily approached the intrigued airport personnel, showing no fear. Miraculously, they had managed to pick him up (without getting bitten) and had placed him in a box in the pilot lounge. Clearly, 186 was not ready to be a wild condor. Former California Condor Recovery Team leader, Lloyd Kiff, once said that "it is normal for scavengers to be attracted to the *activity of lions*; it is not normal for them to be attracted to *the lion*." As Farry aptly noted in his "Notes from the Field" on the Peregrine Fund's Web site in March 1999, "Condor 186, for reasons we do not fully understand, was 'attracted to the lion.'" Farry made the difficult decision to return Condor 186 to captivity.

Eighteen months later, hoping that 186 had matured while in captivity, we decided to give him another chance. On December 29, 2000, this time at the Vermilion Cliffs, we again released Condor 186 to the wild. We were hopeful about 186's chances at making it in the wild, and, for a short time, he met our expectations and stayed out of trouble. Then, to our dismay, 186 discovered the South Rim, a sensory overload for young condors, and his excessive curiosity got the better of him once again. On March 22, 2001, 186 landed repeatedly on RVs that were parked at Grand Canyon's Trailer Village. After a day of trying to haze the troublesome young condor out of the area, Peregrine Fund Condor Project Director, Chris Parish, came upon an unwary Condor 186 preening nonchalantly a few feet from tourists on the rim in

Grand Canyon Village. Frustrated by 186's lack of wariness, Parish sidled up to him by pretending he was a nonthreatening tourist, then reached out and grabbed the unsuspecting bird (receiving a nasty bite in the process). Once again, we returned 186 to captivity.

Despite our frustration, we opted to give Condor 186 one more chance at being a wild condor, releasing him for the fourth time on December 14, 2001, well after the summer tourist season. To our delight, Condor 186 finally did everything right. He stayed away from people at Navajo Bridge, a popular haunt for condors in April and May. He stayed away from rafters in the Colorado River corridor. He stayed away from people at the South Rim. He became proof that even the most curious and unwary of condors can learn to be wild—with the help of multiple time-outs and a lot of additional growing-up time. Throughout the summer, Condor 186 frequented the most remote areas of Grand Canyon and the adjacent Kaibab Plateau. At last, he was focusing on carcasses, not people, the way a wild condor should.

The Kaibab Plateau is a perfect place for a condor. There is plentiful food, a vast forest, cool winds, and dappled shade. With the onset of the fall 2002 hunting season, however, 186's idyllic summer haunts, which had previously been remote and free of people, filled with innumerable camouflage-clad humans. Perched above a deer carcass in the seeming safety of a tree, Condor 186 had no

The Kaibab Plateau is a perfect place for a condor. There is plentiful food, a vast forest, cool winds, and dappled shade.

way of knowing that humans can have a long and dangerous reach. Although he had learned to keep his distance from people, he could not have understood that the one raising a strange object was intent on killing him. Why the hunter loosed an arrow at the condor perched quietly in a ponderosa pine in the Kaibab National Forest will forever remain a mystery. Leaving the condor to bleed to death on the forest floor will forever be his or her shame.

That person's careless gesture was a crime, although the perpetrator was never found. To those of us working with the condors, it was the loss of a troubled young condor that had finally learned to be wild, the loss of a four-year-old whose years of caring for a future generation of condors had been imminent, the loss of a creature whose antics we had railed at and laughed at, and whose successes we had celebrated. Less than two months after 186's death, a bright-eyed and much beloved juvenile, Condor 258, which had exhibited exemplary behavior since his release to the wild in February 2002, also was shot out of a tree on the Kaibab Plateau. Based on the evidence, 258 appears to have been shot with a shotgun by a turkey hunter. His death and the death of Condor 186 marked a very sad time for the field crew.

Shooting

During the course of the reintroduction program, at least five condors have been shot and killed, two in California and three in Arizona. (Some of the condors that disappeared may also have been shot, and at least one more condor in California was shot at, although the shooter missed.) Fortunately, the shooting of a modern-day condor is rare in comparison to the number of condors killed in this way prior to the phasing out of purposeful collection of condors for museum specimens and the enactment of laws prohibiting the shooting of nongame birds

During the course of the reintroduction program, at least five condors have been shot and killed, two in California and three in Arizona.

in the early 1900s, the passing of the Endangered Species Act in 1973, and the increasingly vigorous enforcement of laws protecting nongame birds in the late twentieth century.

The first shooting death of a reintroduced condor in Arizona, which, shockingly, occurred within Grand Canyon National Park, rocked the condor program and devastated those who had followed Condor 124's activities since her release to the wild in May 1997. She had disappeared during the summer following her release and, after going more than thirty days without feeding, showed up dehydrated and emaciated at the South Rim, where she was recaptured and returned to the release site. After a period of rehabilitation at the San Diego Zoo, she was re-released to the wild on September 3, 1997, and she had been remarkably successful—until a university student failed to heed his friends' urgent admonitions not to fire at the big, black bird and took repeated shots at her, killing her.

Multiple years passed without another shooting death in Arizona. During this time period, however, the condor flock began to forage on the Kaibab Plateau with greater frequency. As one of the premier hunting areas in Arizona, the Kaibab receives an enormous influx of hunters each fall, increasing the likelihood that condors would come into contact with gun-toting humans. While most hunters would be appalled by the thought of shooting a condor, and many have contributed to efforts to save the birds, criminals exist in every community. It was two such individuals (neither of whom were ever apprehended) who shot Condor 186 and juvenile Condor 258 in separate incidents during the fall of 2002.

Reeling from the loss of these two birds, the condor program in Arizona mobilized to prevent such senseless killings in the future. Reward offers and informational posters to educate hunters about the presence and protected status of these birds were posted in the Kaibab National Forest and surrounding communities. Beginning in 2003, the Arizona Game and Fish Department (AZGFD) included information about condors with every permit mailed out to hunters. Additionally, the department printed information about condors and their use of the Kaibab Plateau in their hunting regulations handbook. These efforts seem to have made a difference. No condor in Arizona has been lost to shooting since the fall of 2002. Nevertheless, shooting remains the second greatest human threat to condors.

Egg Collecting and Power Line Collisions

Historically, human-caused mortality factors such as shooting, poisoning, and egg collecting, coupled with the California condor's naturally low reproductive rate, nearly resulted in the species' extinction. California condors evolved to live long lives, reproduce slowly, and experience little adult mortality. Their rapid decline in the twentieth century was wholly attributable to an unsustainable level of mortality and mortality factors that indiscriminately targeted breeding adults as well as younger condors. Today, human-caused threats continue to be the greatest risk to the condor's long-term survival. Certain threats have diminished over the last few decades; egg collecting, for instance, has not been an issue in the reintroduction program.

The extent to which utility lines contributed to the decline of condors in the mid- to late 1900s is unknown. Only one instance of a condor colliding with telephone wires was confirmed prior to the reintroduction program (in 1976). However, the loss of seven juvenile condors from collisions or electrocutions in the early years of the reintroduction program (six in California and one in Arizona) suggests this may have been a greater threat to condors than researchers thought (alternatively, the threat of utility line collisions may have been greater for the reintroduced birds because of their stronger attraction to developed areas and human structures compared to their pre-reintroduction counterparts).

In response to these condor deaths, the recovery
program installed electrified mock power poles in
the pre-release pens in both California and Arizona.
Condors landing on modified utility poles received
a mild electric shock, and they learned quickly to
avoid such perches; the method is known as aversive
conditioning. By discouraging the use of power
poles as condor perches, the mock power pole inno-
vation has dramatically reduced both electrocutions
and power-line collisions. Since the institution of
power pole aversion training, no condors in Arizona
and three in California have been killed by power
lines.

In many areas frequented by condors, power
lines that are likely to pose a threat have been retro-
fitted with flappers (hanging plastic tags) and other
devices to make the nearly invisible wires more
noticeable to condors. At the South Rim, for example, all power lines in Grand Canyon Village are
decorated with an array of flappers and coils, and
the tops of poles have been outfitted with perch
guards (triangular pieces of metal) that prevent condors and raptors from landing on these tempting
vantage points. Given the abundance of utility lines
that exists in the condors' range, particularly surrounding the primary release area in southern

California, the low number of collisions in the condor program is truly remarkable and gives hope that condors can indeed survive in a world dominated by the necessities of electricity and high-speed communication.

Poisoning

Historically, poisoning was probably the greatest threat to condors and the primary reason for the precipitous decline of the condor population throughout the 1900s. Poison-laced carcasses meant for scavengers such as coyotes may still be a threat to condors. However, the use of such poisoned bait is less prevalent than it was in the first two-thirds of the twentieth century, when the use of cyanide, strychnine, and compound 1080 was widespread.

Environmental poisons may be an increasing threat to today's condors, particularly because developed areas and the products that inevitably accompany them have dramatically encroached on the condor's range. Indeed, the first fatality in the reintroduction program involved a condor known as Chocuyens ingesting ethylene glycol from an unknown source in October 1992.

Lead poisoning may be the greatest condor mortality factor both historically and currently. Condors and other birds such as eagles and turkey vultures can be exposed to lead by ingesting lead shot or lead bullet fragments from animal carcasses that have been shot. Until the early 1980s, when

biologists outfitted the first condors with radio transmitters, the difficulty of finding dead condors and documenting their cause of death masked how grave a threat lead poisoning was to the birds.

The first wild California condor to wear a radio transmitter was found dead in March 1984. X-rays revealed a bullet fragment in its digestive tract, and subsequent tests showed high levels of lead in its tissues. The following March, a second condor succumbed to lead poisoning. In November 1985, a female condor known as AC-3 was captured, given a routine blood test, and released. Upon discovering that her blood contained high levels of lead, biologists attempted to recapture her. Sadly, researchers were not able to capture her until January, when she was so weak that field personnel were able to run her down and capture her by hand. AC-3 was severely underweight and had rotting food in her crop, indicating that her digestive system was not functioning properly. (One of the most common effects of lead poisoning is the paralysis of the digestive system, which leads to starvation and, eventually, death.) Even after ridding her system of lead, the staff at the San Diego Zoo was unable to alleviate her crop paralysis, and AC-3 died on January 18, 1986.

Despite these alarming mortalities and subsequent studies that showed that 35.8 percent of golden eagles sampled within the condor's range in California had elevated lead levels, some politicians, wildlife managers, conservationists, hunters, and others remained unconvinced of the severity of the threat posed to condors by lead ammunition.

Although some conceded that condors were consuming lead, the source of such lead was disputed. The link between ammunition in carcasses and elevated lead levels in condors seemed tenuous to many, despite X-rays showing a bullet fragment in at least one of the poisoned condors.

Nevertheless, to reduce the exposure of condors to lead, researchers provided food to reintroduced condors in the hopes that they would not forage naturally and encounter lead in carcasses. Despite such precautions, in 1997 biologists found dangerously high lead levels in the blood of three condors released in southern California after they fed on a single hunter-shot deer carcass. Fortunately these three condors were treated and saved, as were three additional condors that suffered lead poisoning in California in 1998.

Spent lead ammunition is known to be widespread in California. A study by Michael Frey, a

Although some conceded that condors were consuming lead, the source of such lead was disputed.

professor at the University of California at Davis, estimated that in 2001, hunters killed 106,049 game animals in the eight counties that comprise the condor's California range. More than 30,000 large animal carcasses and field-dressed visceral remains (gutpiles) are thought to be left in the field annually in this area, including the remains of 8,180 deer, 17,249

wild pigs, and 10,816 coyotes.

Because of the abundant public land in northern Arizona and southern Utah—much of it National Park Service land where hunting is illegal—it was long thought that lead would pose a lesser threat to the Arizona condors than it did for the birds in California. For the first few years of the reintroduction program in Arizona, this belief was validated. However, the death of Condor 116 in Grand Canyon National Park revealed the universality of the lead threat and proved to be an ominous foreshadowing of events to come during the summer of 2000.

Lead Poisoning and the Arizona Condors

At the time of his death at the age of almost five years, Condor 116 was the most dominant and splendid of all the Arizona condors, garnering the field crew's respect for his self-sufficiency and his avoidance of people and developed areas. When Condor 116 landed at a carcass, the other condors made way for him, like a sea of courtiers opening their ranks to allow the passage of royalty. Last seen at the end of January 2000, Condor 116's absence did not alarm the field crew until his radio transmitter began emitting a stationary signal from a remote side canyon on February 9. After weeks of unsuccessful attempts at reaching Condor 116, his body was finally recovered after Field Manager Shawn

Farry, who has the lean physique and mental toughness of the ultramarathoner he once was, hiked a rubber raft down a long, precarious trail into the Grand Canyon, paddled upstream from a spot just above roiling House Rock Rapid, and found 116's body lying undisturbed on the bank of the river. A necropsy conducted by the San Diego Zoo's pathology lab revealed that 116 had died of lead poisoning.

The field crew quickly set about trapping the rest of the Arizona condor flock to test each bird's blood for lead. Because condors are highly gregarious and feed in groups at a carcass, multiple birds are likely to ingest lead if a carcass is contaminated with lead shot or bullet fragments. Discovering that one bird has ingested lead means every bird that fed on the contaminated carcass is also at risk for lead poisoning. Perhaps the greatest tragedy of lead as a mortality factor for condors is that not only does it target multiple birds, but it also inadvertently targets the oldest condors—in population terms, the most valuable members of the flock. Older birds are typically the most dominant, and they are usually the first to access and feed at a carcass. Because condors seek out holes and orifices to begin feeding on the soft tissues of a carcass, a dominant bird may go straight for the wound where a bullet penetrated an animal. In doing so, it is likely to ingest dangerous amounts of lead, because even the highest-quality bullet loses up to 30 percent of its mass, which fragments into microscopic granules on impact and as it passes through the animal. X-rays of deer that died of gunshot wounds have shown an alarming scattering of

The author weighs Condor 203 prior to re-releasing him to the wild. Before returning condors to the wild, biologists weigh and give a health check to each bird that has been treated for lead poisoning.

miniscule lead fragments throughout the animals' body cavities.

After testing the blood of each of the Arizona condors, the condor field crew discovered that Condor 119 also had dangerously elevated lead levels, although she showed no clinical signs of lead poisoning. A second blood test showed that her lead levels were increasing, and she was rushed to the Phoenix Zoo for treatment.

Like the reintroduced condors in California that had been cured of lead poisoning, Condor 119 was saved through a treatment known as chelation therapy. Chelation involves injecting the condor with calcium EDTA, a substance that binds to the lead molecules and allows them to be excreted from the condor's body. A condor with lead poisoning receives an injection in its breast muscle twice a day. The process is uncomfortable for the condor and stressful for both the bird and its handlers. After five days of twice-daily injections, the condor is retested. If its lead values are still high, it must undergo another round of chelation therapy (five more days of twice-daily injections). Once its lead values are within the acceptable range, the condor is held and monitored for another week and then released back to the wild.

Condors seem able to withstand surprisingly high levels of lead without showing any clinical signs of having lead poisoning. Unfortunately, this means that a very sick bird can seem perfectly healthy unless it happens to be subjected to a rou-

tine blood test. Levels of lead in the blood are described either in parts per million (ppm) or in micrograms per deciliter (µg/dL). One ppm is equivalent to 100 µg/dL. In condors, lead levels of less than 0.20 ppm are considered normal due to low levels of lead throughout the condor's environment. Levels of 0.20 to 0.59 ppm mean a condor has been exposed to lead, while a condor with levels of 0.60 to 0.99 ppm is considered clinically affected. A bird with more than 1.00 ppm is diagnosed as having acute lead poisoning.

Although some condors have died with blood-lead levels of a little more than 1.00 ppm, other condors have survived with levels of more than 7.00 ppm. The latter condors most likely would not have lived if intervention and chelation therapy had not followed shortly after they ingested the lead. High doses of lead can kill a condor within a matter of weeks. Lower levels of lead can also kill condors, but do so over a period of months. The condor will experience paralysis of its digestive system and slowly starve to death. More acute lead doses lead to paralysis of the nervous system, leaving a bird unable to walk or fly. Fortunately, Condor 119's lead level of slightly more than 1.00 ppm (compared to Condor 116's level of 3.20 ppm) subsided quickly with chelation therapy, and she was released back to the wild on May 13, 2000.

Although lead affects all birds negatively, condors appear to be more likely to suffer lead poisoning than many other birds in their range for a number of reasons. Unlike birds of prey, which cast, or regurgitate, daily pellets containing the undigested bones and fur of their prey, condors cast pellets more sporadically and are therefore less likely to rid themselves of bullet fragments or pieces of shot before they negatively affect the digestive tract and prevent normal regurgitation. Additionally, because condors typically focus on soft tissues when they feed, they may seek out bone fragments—or other small, hard objects in the carcass—in an attempt to supplement the general lack of calcium in their diet. Finally, the highly acidic digestive systems of condors and other New World Vultures may break lead down more quickly than the systems of many other types of birds. Despite the high levels of lead documented in the blood of some surviving condors in the reintroduction program, condors are considered highly susceptible to lead toxicity. The presence of a single lead shotgun pellet in a condor's gut may be enough to kill the bird.

With the re-release of Condor 119 to the wild and a clean bill of health for the other Arizona condors, the condor field crew returned to business as usual. On June 12, 2000, however, just under a month after 119 returned to the skies, Field Manager Shawn Farry discovered the carcass of Condor 165 at the South Rim. A condor with no history of any behavioral or health problems, three-year-old Condor 165 had last been seen at the South Rim with a number of other condors on June 6. Later that day, he retreated to a cove west of Grand Canyon Village and did not leave the area again. Upon finding 165's body after crisscrossing loose talus slopes on precarious deer trails, Farry realized that 165 had literally dropped off his cliff perch upslope. A necropsy provided an explanation for the bird's abrupt death: twenty lead shotgun pellets in his crop and a blood lead level of more than 3.00 ppm. Once again, the crew set about recapturing all of the Arizona condors.

The worst was yet to come. On June 15, field biologist Gretchen Druliner hiked into the foothills below the Vermilion Cliffs to check on Condor 191, which had been out of view with a stationary radio-transmitter signal near the release area since June 11. It was not long before she found the two-year-old condor huddled under a large rock in the 100°F (38°C) heat. She was emaciated, dehydrated, and heat stressed. Frantically, the crew worked to stabilize her with hydrating fluids. For a while, they were hopeful. But in the middle of the night, she tumbled onto her side, open bill gasping for air. Again the crew provided her with fluids and again she appeared to recover. By morning she was on her feet again, alert and responsive, and the crew transported her to the Phoenix Zoo for additional treatment. X-rays showed no metallic objects in her system, but a blood test showed severe anemia—a symptom of chronic lead poisoning. Urgently, the veterinarians gave her a blood transfusion (using blood from a California condor then in quarantine at the zoo prior to being transferred to the Vermilion Cliffs).

But it was too late; shortly after the transfusion, Condor 191 died.

Four days later, on June 20, Condor 182, another exceptional two-year-old, was found dead in the House Rock Valley below the Vermilion Cliffs release site. She had been absent for nineteen days, and the field crew did not detect her radio-transmitter signal until June 19, when a sharp-eared crewmember heard a faint signal from the valley. Likely, she had been lying in a low area where her radio signal had been blocked for several weeks. Unfortunately, the poor condition of her carcass precluded a necropsy. Nevertheless, given the timing of her death and the similarities between her pre-mortality behavior and that of Condor 191, lead poisoning was suspected.

Before early 2000, each blood sample taken from a condor had to be sent via Federal Express to a lab to be tested for its lead content, and several days passed before the results were faxed to the condor field crew stationed near the Vermilion Cliffs. Fortunately, prior to trapping the entire Arizona flock in the summer of 2000, the field crew acquired a portable lead tester that could provide

results of a bird's lead levels in three minutes rather than in days. This radically improved the crew's speed in recognizing and treating sick condors. The tester only revealed readings of up to 65 μg/dL (0.65 ppm). Any level higher than that was indicated by a reading of "High" on the tester. The blood sample then had to be sent to a lab to get the exact level, but the field tester at least showed whether a bird was lead-free, had low levels of lead, or contained dangerous levels of the toxic substance.

At the end of June 2000, the crew watched anxiously as the 180-second countdown began for the first of their trapped condors. An eternity passed, and still the count plodded downward: 72, 71, 70. . . . Silence reigned. Fingers fidgeted. Everyone stared at the readout, hating the anticipation, but unable to turn away from the inevitable result. Condor 127, a five-year-old female, was on the line. How would she fare? 5, 4, 3, 2, 1, 0. A pause. And then "High" flashed on the screen. Hearts sank, heads dropped momentarily in defeat. But there was no time to waste. Any bird with lead levels more than 45 μg/dL (0.45 ppm) had to be taken for an X-ray at Dr. Jerry Roundtree's veterinary hospital in Page, Arizona—over a two-hour drive on rough roads. While several crewmembers carried the heavy kennel holding 127 up the sandy trail to a waiting vehicle for her trip to the vet, the rest of the crew finished testing the blood-lead levels of the remaining trapped condors. Condors 134 and 193 showed moderate levels of lead

At the **end of June 2000**, the crew watched anxiously as the 180-second countdown began for the first of their trapped condors.

Condor 127 survived lead poisoning and has produced two chicks in the wild thanks to the efforts of the biologists who treated her. Every reintroduced condor wears radio-transmitters on either its wings or tail (one of 127's radio-transmitter antennae is visible near the center of her tail), which allow biologists to monitor the bird's activities, thereby improving its chances of surviving in the wild.

in their systems—they had been exposed and would be monitored closely, their lead levels checked again in a few days to see whether they were increasing. Condor 184 was in the clear. The crew breathed a collective sigh of relief.

Two days later, having trapped several more condors, they watched the agonizing countdown again. This time the screen flashed "High" for Condors 123 and 158. Both were loaded into kennels for transport to the veterinarian. Like Condor 127's radiograph, Condor 123's was negative, showing no sign of the bullet fragments or lead shot that had caused lead to enter his system. Condor 158's radiograph, however, revealed six shotgun pellets in his gizzard. With lead present in his system, his lead levels would continue to rise, as his digestive juices and the grinding action of his gizzard wore away at the pellets. The following morning, July 3, Condor 158 was transported to the Phoenix Zoo.

Two days later, having trapped several more condors, they watched the agonizing countdown again.

X-rays showed that three pellets had moved into his intestines where they would no longer be dissolved and would eventually exit his system, but three remained lodged in his gizzard. Using an endoscope, Drs. Kathy Orr and Curtis Eng were able to remove one of the gizzard pellets, but the other two eluded them. The following day, the two remaining pellets had to be removed surgically. Meanwhile, the veterinarians initiated chelation therapy. Lab results later revealed that Condor 158's blood-lead level had reached 390 µg/dL (3.90 ppm) by the time he underwent surgery. That he is still flying today is testament to the dedication of the field crew and the skill of the veterinarians.

Meanwhile, trapping continued at the Vermilion Cliffs and at the South Rim, and one more condor was lost. On June 21, Condor 150, a four-year-old female that was part of the first group of condors to be released in Arizona in December 1996, left the South Rim and headed back toward the security of the release site, but she never completed her journey. Despite two weeks of extraordinary effort, Farry was never able to recover her body. Lead toxicity could not be confirmed as the cause of death, but given the timing and the situation, it is likely that lead was the culprit.

By the time an exhausted crew captured the last of the free-flying condors on July 13, nine of the sixteen birds in the wild had been diagnosed as having lead poisoning. X-rays revealed lead pellets in the digestive tracts of four condors (including 158). Condors 119 and 136 passed their respective shotgun pellets unaided. However, Condor 133 needed assistance from the veterinarians, eventually passing hers only after having her gizzard repeatedly flushed with water. All nine birds with lead poisoning received chelation therapy—a major production for the condor field crew, who had to net each bird in the flight pen twice daily to give them the requisite injections—and three of the birds required a second round of chelation. All birds receiving chelation therapy survived. Nonetheless, by the end of the summer, the Arizona condor population had been diminished by five—almost one quarter of the Arizona condors had been lost over the course of two lead incidents.

For a time, the devastating events of the summer of 2000 were viewed as anomalous. To a degree, recent history has supported this view, because the lead that has subsequently killed condors has come from lead bullet fragments rather than lead shotgun pellets. The source of the lead pellets in 2000 remains a mystery. How a large enough carcass to feed at least ten birds came to be riddled with the two sizes of shotgun pellets found in the birds' digestive tracts is anyone's guess. Large animals are usually killed with bullets, not shotgun shells. Perhaps someone idly peppered an already-dead range cow with a shotgun. Or maybe someone piled up a large number of rabbit or coyote carcasses, unaware of the devastating effect this offal could have on scavengers.

Fortunately, the condor reintroduction program has not seen a repetition of the events of the summer of 2000. Unfortunately, lead has continued to be the greatest threat to condors in Arizona. Eighteen-month-old Condor 240, a magnificent

For a time, the devastating events of the summer of 2000 were viewed as anomalous.

flier and highly capable juvenile, succumbed to lead poisoning in August 2002. Aggressive, feisty, independent, and endearingly ungraceful Condor 235, a five-year-old female, died of lead toxicity in January 2005. Condor 249, another stellar flier and model young condor, died within two weeks of Condor 235, having fed on the same carcass.

Amidst these fatalities were many more condors saved through countless rounds of chelation, an untold number of X-rays, and numerous trips to the Phoenix Zoo. Showing a remarkable ability to find and feed on natural carcasses, the Arizona condors did what everyone had hoped of them—became wild, self-sufficient creatures—but in doing so, they put themselves at constant risk. Lead poisoning became more prevalent as the condors discovered the bounty of the Kaibab Plateau and its district of the Kaibab National Forest during the hunting season. In 2001 alone, 3,967 tags were provided to hunters and an estimated 2,164 gutpiles and 268 unrecovered carcasses were left in the condor's range in Arizona. Such a bounty could be an extraordinarily beneficial source of food for condors were it not for the fact that so many of these gutpiles and carcasses contained lead.

As the condor flock spent more and more of its time on the Kaibab Plateau and its environs each fall, the number of Arizona condors showing elevated lead levels climbed steadily. In the fall of 2002, twelve condors (39 percent of the population) had to receive chelation therapy to rid their systems of lead (four of these required two rounds of chelation). The fall of 2003 was somewhat anomalous, as we decided to trap and hold as many birds as we could in the safety of our large flight pen during the hunting season to minimize their exposure to lead. Of the thirty-three condors free-flying in Arizona at the time, a total of seventeen condors were trapped and held during the course of the fall. Eight of these required chelation to save them from lead poisoning. Most of the sixteen condors that remained in the wild eluded capture, and their lead levels went untested. During the fall hunting season of 2004, no birds were held during

To minimize the Arizona condor flock's exposure to lead, the field crew provides the condors with a steady supply of calf carcasses at the release site.

the hunting season, and a staggering 85 percent (thirty-five of forty-one) of the free-flying condors in Arizona showed lead exposure during the hunting season. Eighteen condors received chelation therapy, five of which required two rounds.

Elevated lead levels outside the hunting season were uncommon. However, several sightings of condors feeding on shot coyote carcasses each summer led the field crew to recapture the birds; ensuing blood tests revealed high levels of lead, X-rays showed ingested bullet fragments, and timely chelation therapy managed to restore the birds to apparent good health. The long-term effects of repeated lead exposures, chronically low lead levels, and chelation therapy itself are unknown.

To minimize the Arizona condor flock's exposure to lead, the field crew provides the condors with a steady supply of calf carcasses at the release site. Surprisingly, the abundance of available food has not stopped the condors from finding and feeding on naturally occurring carcasses. Peregrine Fund and Grand Canyon National Park personnel documented a total of 130 animal carcasses found by condors in 2002 and 2003. However, the supplemental food provided by the field crew helps reduce the condors' exposure to potentially contaminated carcasses.

In addition to providing supplementary carcasses, the field crew routinely tests the entire Arizona condor flock for lead during the hunting season and throughout the year when the opportunity arises. Any condor seen feeding on a dead animal that is suspected of having been shot is recaptured as quickly as possible, tested for lead, and treated if necessary. Any coyote carcass found by the field crew is disposed of immediately, because it is legal

Over the last few years, nonlead ammunition has become increasingly available, and a growing number of hunters are using nonlead alternatives in condor country. The least harmful bullets currently available for game on which scavengers are likely to feed are made of copper. Copper bullets do not fragment upon impact, whereas lead bullets can lose as much as 30 percent of their mass upon impact, leaving a scatter of minute lead fragments in the carcass. In addition to resisting fragmentation, copper bullets are less toxic to wildlife than lead bullets. Copper-jacketed bullets, although an improvement over all-lead bullets, are still problematic in that they contain a highly toxic lead core that is prone to fragmentation.

High-performance, all-copper bullets are now available in most rifle calibers. Shotgun, pistol, and muzzleloader ammunition is also available in high-performance, nonlead alternatives. There are even nonlead alternatives for hand-loaders.

The Arizona Game and Fish Department (AZGFD) has made extraordinary efforts to educate Arizona hunters about the threat of lead to condors and to supply concrete documentation of this threat in their annual hunter regulation handbook. On their Web site (http://www.azgfd.gov) and in the handbook, the agency provides both a comprehensive list of nonlead ammunition in a wide range of calibers and a list of distributors that carry these bullets. Furthermore, AZGFD recommends that hunters use nonlead ammunition within the condor's range in Arizona. Hunters not wishing to use nonlead ammunition are encouraged to remove all shot animals (including coyotes) from the field and to remove their gutpiles or bury them with rocks and brush. If leaving animals or gutpiles in the field, hunters are asked to consider removing bullets and the flesh surrounding the wound.

In the fall of 2005, AZGFD offered coupons to the 2,393 hunters who drew deer permits for the Kaibab Plateau, which they could redeem at selected national sporting goods stores for two boxes of nonlead ammunition. The coupons were accompanied by information regarding the threat of lead to condors. Roughly 65 percent of hunters redeemed their coupons, showing an extraordinary level of interest in conserving wildlife through the use of nonlead ammunition.

The recent efforts of AZGFD to encourage the voluntary use of nonlead ammunition while still respecting hunters' rights to make their own choices are an unprecedented, encouraging, and much-needed step toward securing a safe future for Arizona's condors.

Copper bullets do not fragment upon entering their target as lead bullets do (intact copper bullet, right; copper bullet retrieved after having been shot, left) and are less toxic to wildlife. Because they maintain their integrity, copper bullets are less likely to be ingested by scavengers feeding on a shot animal.

to shoot coyotes year-round in the condor's range (outside of the national park), and the lead ammunition typically used to kill them is especially prone to fragmenting.

Although recognition and acceptance of this threat has been slow, changes are beginning to happen. In California, efforts by organizations such as Project Gutpile, a group of hunters and biologists who support the use of nonlead bullets and responsible hunting practices, have helped raise awareness of the lead problem. Such efforts may be helping by educating hunters about the effects of lead, convincing them to bury the remains of animals they shoot, and encouraging them to use nonlead ammunition.

In 2003 the California Condor Recovery Team and the U.S. Fish and Wildlife Service (USFWS) contracted a consulting group to conduct surveys of hunters to determine the most effective way of getting the "lead message" out to hunters. The goal was to not alienate those who feared the passage of the same type of legislation that outlawed the use of lead shot for waterfowl hunting when few effective alternatives were available (this is no longer the case). In Arizona, the AZGFD followed up on the findings of these surveys by sending out information on lead and condors with all permits mailed to hunters beginning in 2003. In 2004 the hunting regulation handbook published by the agency included two pages highlighting the scientific evidence on the threat of lead to condors. In addition, the AZGFD asked hunters for their voluntary help in burying gutpiles and provided them with a list of all nonlead ammunition currently available. Such an unprecedented effort by a state game agency gives reason to hope that hunters will increasingly opt for nonlead alternatives, and that, in doing so, they will create a growing market for nonlead ammunition, ensuring that the cost will be acceptable to the average hunter.

Watching the condors settle in on the Vermilion Cliffs one fall evening in 2003, I was joined by a father and son, both dressed in camouflage and sporting smiles that could only mean they had had a successful hunt on the Kaibab Plateau. After shooting his first-ever deer, the young boy, who evidently was a raptor and condor aficionado, had begged his father to stop at the condor release area so he could get a look at the giant birds that heretofore had graced only his books and his imagination. As we talked, I hesitantly tried to tell them how beneficial the remains of their deer, left in the forest up on the Kaibab, could be to the condors—if only it didn't contain lead. "Well, that's why we shot with Barnes X [a brand of nonlead ammunition] this year," the father responded. "We didn't want to hurt the condors." My smile that night surely rivaled those of the

Although recognition and acceptance of this threat has been slow, changes are beginning to happen. ✑

man and boy who were doing their vital part in helping me look out for condors.

West Nile Virus

Although human-caused mortality factors will likely determine whether or not the California condor will survive in the modern world, condors in the reintroduction program have also perished from natural causes. One threat that thus far has not led to condor mortalities in Arizona—but has the potential of doing so—is West Nile Virus. Carried to the United States in 1999, this mosquito-borne virus has killed birds representing at least 138 species, including the condor's close relative, the turkey vulture. Fortunately, an experimental vaccine developed by the Centers for Disease Control and Prevention (CDC) that is safer and more effective than the vaccine developed for horses showed early promising results for two crow species. The CDC willingly agreed to include condors in its evaluation of the vaccine. Accordingly, in 2003, eight Andean and twenty-seven California condors were vaccinated twice, twenty-one days apart. When no side effects from the vaccine were documented on these captive birds, condor release programs in California, Arizona, and Baja California recaptured and vaccinated all of their free-flying wild condors. Although the level of protection provided by the vaccine remains uncertain, thus far no vaccinated California condor has perished from the virus.

Sadly though, a three-month-old, unvaccinated, wild-hatched chick that died in California in August 2005 tested positive for West Nile Virus, the first California condor to do so. Because nest caves in the wild are often difficult to access, it had not yet been vaccinated. Tests on progeny of vaccinated captive condors showed that maternal immunity to the disease was transferred to chicks. However, the longevity of such immunity had not yet been determined. With the death of the chick, biologists now believe that the maternal West Nile Virus antibodies inherited by the chick wore off at just over a month of age. While zoo personnel will continue to investigate how long maternal antibodies transferred to chicks may last, field biologists will attempt to vaccinate wild-hatched condors while they are still in their nest caves to prevent future losses to the virus.[9]

Natural Enemies: Golden Eagles and Coyotes

California condors have few natural enemies aside from humans. Although ravens have been known to destroy and eat their eggs, the inaccessibility of most condor nests ensures that chicks are rarely if ever lost to predators. Adult condors similarly experience

[9] *In July 2006, four three-month-old captive condor chicks that had not been vaccinated for West Nile Virus died of the disease at the World Center for Birds of Prey in Boise, Idaho.*

A golden eagle prepares to land at a carcass near two juvenile condors at the Vermilion Cliffs release site. Golden eagles have killed several newly released condors. Older condors frequently chase eagles away from the release area and away from nest sites.

little to no predation, although numerous nonfatal attacks by eagles have been documented both historically and during the course of the reintroduction program. However, newly released condors have shown themselves to be vulnerable to golden eagle and coyote predation. These predators have killed as many as eight condors in Arizona alone.

The first Arizona fatality occurred in January 1997, when Condor 142, part of the first cohort of birds to be released at the Vermilion Cliffs, was killed by a golden eagle a month after being released. Condor 197 was also killed by an eagle a mere two months after her December 1999 release from the Hurricane Cliffs. As newly released condors improve their flight skills, becoming more agile and confident in the air, they appear to become less vulnerable to golden eagles, which are thought to target condors because they perceive them as competitors (as opposed to food items). Juvenile condors quickly learn that they cannot elude golden eagles in the air and are safest if they retreat to the shelter of a cliff or slope. Fortunately, with the presence of increasing numbers of adult condors (which readily chase off golden eagles) at the Vermilion Cliffs release site, the threat of golden eagles to newly released condors appears to have diminished. No condor has been killed by a golden eagle since at least September 2000.

While the threat of golden eagles to young condors appears to have decreased in Arizona, biologists frequently witness aggressive interactions between the two species. Field crewmembers have watched golden eagles attempt to drive condors off a carcass by repeatedly diving at them or by grabbing at them with a taloned foot when the two birds are on a carcass or on the ground. Likewise, condors have been seen snapping at golden eagles with their bills or jumping at or onto them aggressively to dislodge them from a carcass or perch. On one comic, albeit nerve-wracking occasion, I watched Condor 114 run repeatedly up a steep slope to chase off a golden eagle each time it tried to land. Because of the vulnerability of young, inexperienced condors to golden eagles, however, the field crew at the release area fires a noisemaker to scare off any eagle that is aggressively pursuing a newly released condor.

Coyotes are perhaps the greatest threat to newly released condors in Arizona and are second only to lead poisoning in the number of reintroduced condor deaths they have caused. Fortunately, a very dedicated condor field crew has worked to consistently mitigate this threat. The vulnerability of inexperienced young condors to coyotes is likely

tied to juveniles' limited flight skills. Upon leaving the release pen for the first time, some young condors find it difficult to land on the sheer cliff face where the older condors typically roost for the night. Unable to stall and slow their flight enough to land on a narrow cliff ledge, they often overshoot their target. If unable to land on the cliff face, they must then either fly higher to land on the cliff rim or drop down to land on the talus slope below the cliff. Unfortunately, they are vulnerable to coyotes if they opt to sleep in either of these two places.

Condors are reluctant to fly at night and can be sound sleepers. They often sleep lying down as geese do, with their head tucked under a wing. If they sleep in a spot accessible to coyotes, they risk being killed during the night. Wild juvenile condors are less susceptible to nighttime predation than reintroduced juveniles, because predators are unlikely to be abundant in the area that a newly fledged condor happens to land. In contrast, at the release site, the almost continuous presence of calf carcasses attracts a host of predators (coyotes, bobcats, and at least one mountain lion).

The vulnerability of newly released condors was brought home to me shortly after I joined the condor program as Field Manager in December 2000.

Wild condors learn survival skills over many years. Released to the wild as an eight-year-old, captive-reared Condor 82 revealed her ignorance of predators by perching on small rock outcrops on the valley floor instead of on the safety of the cliffs. This photograph was taken on the day before coyotes killed Condor 82.

On Christmas Day 2000, I headed out with my radio-tracking equipment to find nine-year-old Condor 82, one of the newly released adults. The day before, she had flown north of the release site and, in her inexperience, had failed to maintain elevation and dropped into the foothills below the Vermilion Cliffs. A crewmember hazed Condor 82 onto a seemingly safe rock outcropping, but she had to leave the condor when darkness made further hazing impossible. I knew I was close to where Condor 82 had roosted the night before when her radio-transmitter signal began booming loudly through my receiver (the louder the signal, the closer the condor), but looking around I didn't see her. Instead, I saw the imprint of a condor's wings in the fresh snow. Condor 82 had been perched on the ground when something had caused her to attempt to get airborne quickly. My pulse sped into

Just before my arrival, the Peregrine Fund had experimented with the release of two captive adult birds. The hope was that if these birds could make it in the wild, we would not have to wait the six years it takes a condor to reach maturity before they started to breed. Sadly though, the two adults were ill equipped to cope in the wild.

double-time as the nature of that something became instantly apparent: coyote tracks were all over the snow, surrounding the fragile imprint of the large bird's wings.

I walked on a few steps and found a few small condor feathers. The coyotes had nipped at her as she struggled to escape, detaching some of her feathers. A few steps farther on, I found a flight feather, a tail feather, and scratch marks in the snow. Perhaps one coyote had grabbed her tail and another caught hold of her wing. No matter the scenario, her efforts to fly free had been unsuccessful. Panicked now, her feet had dug deep into the snow and the sand beneath it. I took a few more steps and saw the increased urgency of her struggles: more feathers, deeper scratch marks in the snow, and finally, pitched battle. The snow was churned up, orange with the sand that it had covered. Small branches from the surrounding bushes had been snapped off. Deep grooves like those of a heavily used cutting board rent the snow and sand. Outside this disrupted circle, this vestige of the last desperate struggle for life, a drag mark like a toboggan track disappeared over an embankment. Mouth dry, eyes wide, pulse skipping, heart aching, I followed the track, hating to see what I knew I would find. Down a small drainage, I found Condor 82's badly scavenged body, discarded after being dragged there and fed upon by coyotes. It was my first condor fatality. Condor 82 had fought for life with everything she had. Sickened by her final failed battle, I vowed to do no less: I would do everything I could to prevent this kind of loss again.

But before I had recovered from the shock and sadness of Condor 82's death, her mate, Condor 74, died in the same way—less than a week later. At the time, we had not even realized that he was vulnerable, because he had roosted up on the cliff rim at the release site. His death taught us that roosting on the cliff rim was as unsafe as roosting on small rock outcroppings in the valley. The birds needed to be on the cliff *face*, not on the accessible surface above the cliff, to avoid the dangers that prowled after dark. From that point on, I made sure no condors were ever left to roost on the cliff rim again. Just before roost every night, a crewmember would patrol the cliff, checking every bird's radio signal and determining its location to ensure that each condor was perched safely on the cliff face and not up on the rim. Any bird trying to roost on the rim was hazed into flight, forcing it to seek inaccessible perches. If it returned to the rim, it was hazed again until it finally landed on the cliffs. No more condors succumbed to coyotes on the cliff rim.

Unfortunately, we still had more to learn about protecting condors from coyotes. This time, it was newly released juvenile Condor 252 that inadvertently taught us this lesson. Only a few days after his release in February 2002, Condor 252 eluded us at roost time. We knew from our radio-telemetry that he was not on the rim, yet, despite extensive searching with spotting scopes and binoculars, we could not find him. Bad weather and poor visibility conspired against us. Vainly, we hoped he had tucked himself in out of view in a crevice on the face of the Vermilion Cliffs.

When his signal remained stationary for two days, I feared the worst. No one had been able to spot him from the valley. Carefully, I walked the cliff rim, leaning out precariously to see if I could spot him on a hidden ledge. And then I saw what looked like a wing—a detached wing—with what appeared to be a numbered tag. Shaken, saddened, I radioed down what I thought I was seeing to crewmember Kevin Fairhurst. With an alacrity born of fierce dedication to his work and to the condors, Fairhurst climbed the nearly vertical talus slope, rocks and stones falling away below him, and scaled

Condors were never again allowed to roost on the talus slope at the base of the cliff.

the small bands of cliffs that crisscrossed the slope. Little remained of Condor 252. To our dismay, we also discovered bones from the carcasses that we fed the condors on the rim littering the base of the cliff where Condor 252 had been killed by coyotes that had been drawn to this food bonanza. We had never considered the consequences of the condors inadver-

tently dragging a carcass over the cliff edge as they tugged on it while feeding. Now the coyote tracks and scat that surrounded the discarded bones and 252's scavenged body made those consequences clear. Once again, we adapted.

From that point on, carcasses were bolted onto large rocks on the cliff rim, and any remains were removed and disposed of to prevent them from falling over the cliff edge. Condors were never again allowed to roost on the talus slope at the base of the cliff. What had seemed like an epic climb by Fairhurst eventually became a routine hike for virtually everyone on the crew. If a young bird tried unsuccessfully to land on the cliff and defaulted to landing on the talus, a crewmember made the arduous hike up and hazed the condor repeatedly until it moved to a safe spot. The hazing had the dual purpose of moving a condor to safety and teaching it that if it perched in an unsafe place, it would be pursued by a frustratingly persistent and frightening predator.

At times we wondered about our sanity. No longer did we give up once it got dark. More nights than I care to remember, crewmembers crossed and recrossed the sheer, unstable talus below the release area, with only headlamps lighting the way, trying to move a reluctant condor to a safe roost spot. Handheld radios and the beams from our headlamps united and coordinated our efforts. If a vulnerable condor could not be forced to move to safety, we switched gears and tried to recapture it. After being placed in a transport kennel and returned to the safety of the release pen, it would be rereleased at a later date and given another chance. Ultimately, all newly released condors learned how to roost safely and avoid the four-legged (and two-legged) beasts that prowled at night.

Condor 241, a woefully submissive juvenile condor, made us raise the bar even higher on the measures we would take to keep a condor alive at night. On wobbly wings, she attempted to perch safely on the cliff with the older condors shortly after being released to the wild in December 2002. But, as with so many juvenile condors in the days immediately following their release, she defaulted to the talus slope just before the last light faded from the sky. We spent hours trying to haze her to a safe perch. Attempts to recapture her similarly failed. If we could just get her through the first few nights, her flight skills would improve enough for her to land safely on the cliff. Exhausted and frustrated, we paused in our efforts and regrouped. What to do now? I was unwilling to leave her, stubborn in my determination to protect every condor I could. Hesitantly, I asked "Anyone want to spend the night out here with her?" Although my tone was half joking, I was dead serious, although I hated to ask such a thing of the crew. It was close to freezing. Staying with her would mean sleeping outside in the middle of winter on the side of what most people would classify as a cliff. Had I not been ill at the time, I would have insisted on doing it myself. Fortunately, though, crewmember Ty Donnelly quickly volunteered.

Donnelly and another crewmember remained near Condor 241 all night—close enough to ward off potential predators, far enough away to keep from habituating the vulnerable young condor. Other crewmembers spent the night in our tent "up top" and in trucks in the valley to ensure that those sleeping on the cliffs were only a radio call from help should they need it. A few days later, Condor 241 began roosting safely on the cliff face. She had made it through her most vulnerable period and would grace the skies and land effortlessly on cliff ledges for years to come.

Not everyone agreed with these methods. Over the years, for every biologist who stepped up without hesitation to do whatever it took to help a condor in need, there was another who balked, who decried these "irresponsible methods," who complained bitterly about this obsessive determination to get each condor over that one hurdle that would ensure its survival.

However, while some disagreed with the use of such extreme measures, few could argue with the results. As of the time that this book went to press, no condor in Arizona had been lost to a coyote since Condor 252's death in February 2002. Now all field crewmembers in Arizona, California, and Baja California haze inexperienced young condors to safety after dark and, if need be, hunker down nearby in sleeping bags to get condors through the one night that might mean the difference between death and survival.

AC-8
(~1976–2003)

Only four condors remained in the wild in early 1986. AC-8 (for Adult Condor #8) was the only female. Having lost her original mate, she chose the youngest of the three remaining males, six-year-old AC-9, as her new mate. The pair produced an egg in April that was taken almost immediately by biologists to be incubated and raised in captivity. On the very day their egg hatched at the San Diego Wild Animal Park, June 6, 1986, AC-8 herself was captured to become a member of the same captive flock as her new hatchling.

AC-8 spent the next fourteen years of her life in captivity, producing nine offspring with AC-5, the mate with whom she was paired for genetic reasons. After 1995, however, AC-8 stopped laying eggs. Soon an upwelling of support for releasing her back to the wild took shape within the condor program. If she could not reproduce in captivity, why not release her back to the wild in the hopes that she would serve as a mentor for the young condors that were now flying free in southern California? Accordingly, on April 4, 2000, AC-8 was released from her temporary holding enclosure in a remote corner of the Sespe Condor Sanctuary and once again embraced freedom. She wore the first satellite transmitter ever worn by a California condor.

To everyone's delight, AC-8 adapted easily to life back in the wild, a remarkable feat for a creature that had been confined to a pen for more than a decade. Within weeks, she was revisiting her old haunts and, in time, was followed to these places by young condors that had never thought to venture there before. According to Bruce Palmer, then Condor Coordinator for the USFWS, AC-8 was giving the youngsters "something we could not. . . . She was keeping condor traditions alive."[10]

In November of 2001, AC-8 was recaptured for a routine blood test and transmitter replacement. To the dismay of the USFWS field crew, AC-8's blood contained alarming levels of lead. X-rays showed a discernible metal fragment in her digestive tract and, over the next few days, her blood-lead levels soared. AC-8 could not eat. She would not drink. Frantically, the stellar veterinary staff at the Los Angeles Zoo worked to save her. She was repeatedly chelated (treated for lead poisoning), force-fed, and hydrated. It was a month before the veterinarians could finally say that AC-8, miraculously, had recovered.

With great trepidation, the USFWS rereleased AC-8 in late December 2002. While everyone desperately wanted to keep her safe, no one wanted to see her die in captivity. Any questions about whether AC-8 belonged in the wild were put to rest as she bolted out of her transport kennel and flapped back into the sky. If she could avoid carcasses containing lead bullet fragments, her future looked promising.

But on February 8, 2003, a twenty-nine-year-old man hunting on a Kern County ranch with his father raised his gun and fired a bullet through AC-8's body. The bullet exited through her wing, and AC-8 fell into a fork in the oak tree that had been her final perch. The man claimed he didn't know that he was shooting a condor despite the bird's iconic presence in California.

---

[10] *Quoted in* New Scientist *176 (5 October 2002): 34.*

With this careless gesture, this thoughtless crime, the man did a grave disservice to countless Californians and condor aficionados who mourned AC-8 as they would have a friend, who raged at the senselessness of her loss, who eulogized her in every form of media. His action unfairly tainted the reputation of true hunters who do not kill indiscriminately and have supported efforts to protect condors. The shooting of AC-8 was an affront to the early conservationists who fought to keep AC-8 in the wild, knowing the concept of wilderness would be infinitely compromised without her presence; to scientists who fought to bring AC-8 into captivity, knowing it was the only way to keep her safe and to keep her kind flying into the future; to impassioned condor biologists, old and new, who fought to return her to the sky; and to a new generation of condors that might have benefited from her experience and her knowledge.

AC-8's progeny fly free in Arizona and California. She has left a legacy of more than twenty condors in Arizona alone. AC-8 was an icon that transcended the condor program, a link to what once was, a reminder of our failings, and a hope for what we could become.

AC-8 powers her way back into the wild after a prolonged treatment for a nearly fatal dose of lead. The last female condor remaining in the wild in 1986, AC-8 was captured to become a member of the captive-breeding program that ultimately helped save her species. She was returned to the wild after fourteen years in captivity.

7 Wild Condors, Once Again

....

ℭ Perhaps one of the more difficult aspects of trying to restore a long-lived, slowly reproducing species is that nothing happens quickly. In 2001 condor recovery seemed to be progressing at a glacial pace. The first condors had been reintroduced to the wild in California in 1992 and in Arizona in 1996, but none had started reproducing, despite the fact that a few reintroduced condors had reached maturity. No California condors had nested in the wild since 1986, the year before the last wild condors were captured and brought into captivity.

Seeing California condors once again flying free over northern Arizona and southern Utah, including this condor soaring above the Grand Canyon's Plateau Point Trail, has thrilled wildlife biologists. But condor researchers knew that the survival of the species ultimately depended on condors reproducing in the wild.

The oldest reintroduced condors in Arizona were a year younger than their California counterparts, so those involved in the reintroduction effort in Arizona watched the activities in California with impatient eyes, hoping that an egg laid in California would mean that we could soon expect the same in Arizona. In the spring of 2000, two six-year-old male condors in California began courtship displays to females. Subsequently, one pair of condors disappeared repeatedly into a remote canyon. Although biologists suspected the pair was searching out nest caves, they were unable to confirm whether or not the pair had laid an egg before the two condors stopped frequenting the canyon and rejoined the rest of the flock.

The First Egg

Perched high atop an exposed cliff, the Colorado River tumbling past far below me in a silence borne of distance, I made myself comfortable, adjusted my spotting scope, and sighed in contentment. I was in one of my favorite condor viewing spots, surrounded by wind and emptiness, a distant speck to the birds whose activities I was documenting. It was

my good fortune that day to monitor a trio of adults that teetered on the threshold of maturity. I was also keeping a sharp lookout for an errant young condor that had recently left the release site for the first time since his return to the wild after an extended bout in captivity. It was an ordinary day in Arizona Condorland: Sunday, March 21, 2001.

For days now, those of us working with the condors in Arizona had taken turns staring at a cliff that forms the downstream side of Badger Canyon, a side canyon that runs perpendicular to the Colorado River in the Grand Canyon. A ledge, which is partially obscured by a natural rock wall, runs just below an overhang midway down the sheer sandstone cliff. Over the last few days, six-year-old Condors 119, 123, and 127 had been disappearing into the space behind this wall for extended stretches of time. They seemed to be honing in on a suitable nest location.

Field biologists in Arizona had a foreshadowing of things to come in September 2000, when male Condor 123 suddenly extended his great wings, pointed his wing tips toward the ground, drooped his head, and rocked back and forth from one foot to another while facing female Condor 119. It was a dance that looked as ungainly as it did noble. We were witnessing our first condor courtship display.

To the delight of the Arizona field crew, Condor 123's displays to 119 were soon followed by another type of breeding behavior: the tandem flights and aerial tail-chases known as "synchronized flight." During these breathtakingly beautiful flights, one breeding-age condor flies close to another and shadows the lead bird so closely that the two seem to move as one. The flights evoke grace and power, speed and synchrony. Typically seen in the fall, these flights are thought to be indicative of impending courtship, a type of pair-bonding or pair-maintenance behavior that generally will be followed by nesting in the months to come.

Condor 119 and 123's first tandem flight on September 9 was followed minutes later by a sure sign that the birds had come of age: nest searching. For the first time, despite it being as familiar a part of their landscape as the release pen or the Colorado River, the two birds became interested in a small cave high in the face of the Vermilion Cliffs. Repeatedly the two disappeared inside.

Now, in March, the two had broadened their horizons, investigating this more suitable nest site in Badger Canyon. Unfortunately, the pair had been joined by a third bird, female Condor 127. With limited options in a population of near-adults that

Condors 123 (left) and 127 (right), a breeding pair, fly together over Grand Canyon. During the fall, adult condors may perform "synchronized flights." These ritualized flights, in which one bird closely shadows the other's aerial maneuvers, are usually followed by nest-searching and, ultimately, egg-laying.

numbered only three males and three females, 127 sought out the most dominant male, Condor 123, and kept close to him. Condor 123, while focusing his attentions primarily on 119, also began displaying to and associating with 127, particularly as 119 spent more and more time in the Badger Canyon nest cave. Although we could not see it, she was likely "nest grooming." When condors are investigating possible nest sites, they will smooth the surface of the cave floor with their bills, pushing around small pebbles and debris to prepare a safe depression for the placement of their egg. Lying down, they may also pull sand around them and sift it over their backs, eventually forming a protective circle of material that will help keep a future egg in place.

Trained on the Badger cave, my spotting scope now revealed Condors 123 and 127 loafing at the nest entrance. Condor 119 had been out of view in the cave for over an hour and a quarter. Suddenly, the recently released Condor 198 flew into view coming down the drainage then alighted next to Condors 123 and 127. Chaos erupted. Not liking an intruder in the vicinity of their nest, the older condors quickly rallied to drive off 198. Condor 119 came charging out of her cave, whereupon 123 turned on her, in a brief and seemingly misplaced bout of aggression, before the two focused on Condor 198. The three adults finally drove 198 out of the area and returned to the nest ledge, whereupon 123 disappeared into the cave. When he

emerged nine minutes later, he appeared to be pushing something around with his bill.

"Another bout of nest grooming," I thought to myself. But as 123 stepped away from the nest, I saw that he had actually been pushing around a large, smooth, elliptical object that looked just like . . . an *egg*! A condor egg! Frantically, I tried to focus my scope for a closer look, but it was already zoomed in. I sat as still as a stone, barely breathing, my mind racing. Had there been a smooth white rock at the cave entrance earlier? Surely I would have noted it. I struggled to contain my excitement but remained outwardly calm, bent on being absolutely sure of what I was seeing. This news was too big to risk making a mistake. If I was looking at an actual egg, it would be the first documented condor egg laid in the wild in fifteen years and the first egg laid by re-introduced condors. Carefully, I recorded everything I was seeing in my field notebook. For almost an hour I stared at the beautifully smooth object.

While I watched, Condor 119 left the area, and 123 spent a few minutes in the nest before joining 127 on the ledge adjacent to the nest entrance. Finally, 127 walked over to the possible egg, then, reaching down, placed her bill inside its hollowed out end. I was elated! It was indeed a condor egg. No rock could be so smooth, elliptical, white, and hollow to boot. But quick on the heels of elation came disappointment. The egg was *hollow*, empty, devoid of the vital fluids that might have nourished a developing condor chick. The condors (most likely Condor 119) had indeed laid an egg. But the nest attempt had failed; the precious egg lay broken.

Nonetheless, the sighting of the egg was major news in the conservation world. None of us had expected the birds to successfully hatch an egg on their first attempt. Condors rarely succeed in producing a fertile egg in their first year of breeding and if they do so, they rarely manage to hatch it successfully the first time around. The broken egg in no way diminished the extraordinary fact that a pair of young condors, raised in captivity and released to the wild as two-year-olds, had found a suitable nest cave high in a cliff and laid their first egg.

A Nestling in California

Events in California during the spring of 2001 were at least as exciting as those unfolding in Arizona but, sadly, had similarly disappointing conclusions. As in Arizona, a trio of birds proved to be unsuccessful in their nesting attempt. In California, however, two eggs were laid in a cave in Santa Barbara County's Lion Canyon, and all three "parents" took turns at incubating them. On June 1 U.S. Fish and Wildlife Service (USFWS) and Los Angeles Zoo personnel rappelled down to the nest to examine the eggs to determine whether or not they were viable. One egg was dead, although it had been fertile, and the other was developing but was in poor condition. The team collected both eggs in the hopes of resuscitating the

Around June 21, a condor nestling broke through its shell and became the first California condor chick to hatch in the wild since 1986. ☙

ailing embryo in captivity and left a dummy egg in the nest. The presence of a single fake egg would focus the trio's efforts on incubating one egg and would allow them to keep gaining valuable incubating experience. Ultimately, the wild-laid egg was incubated and hatched successfully in captivity.

When the wild trio's dummy egg was due to hatch (had it been a real egg), the team replaced the artificial egg with a ready-to-hatch egg that had been laid by captive birds at the Los Angeles Zoo. Such manipulations were carried out to give the young condors as much experience as possible with incubating, hatching, and (hopefully) raising a nestling, to help jump-start reproduction in the wild.

Around June 21, a condor nestling broke through its shell and became the first California condor chick to hatch in the wild since 1986. Sadly, though, the trio situation again conspired against a successful nesting attempt. Condors typically incubate for two to four days before ceding the duty to their mate (although condors in Arizona have been documented doing stints as long as nine days before being relieved). Because a baby condor typically takes three days to emerge from its egg, both parents are usually present at some time during the transformation from egg to nestling. In the case of the California trio, however, having two birds to keep each other company while the third incubated reduced each member of the trio's anxiety to get back to the nest to take over incubation. Female Condor 111, which witnessed the hatching of the chick, had been in the nest for more than a week before male Condor 100 and female Condor 108 finally returned to take a turn at incubating. Condor 111 flew out to join the errant pair, and 108 dropped down to the cave to take over incubation duty. Instead of finding her egg, however, 108 was greeted by a puzzling little "invader." Not understanding that this intruder had come from *inside* the egg, she pushed it out of the nest, likely in an attempt to return the nest cave to its familiar status. (Similar behavior had been observed in inexperienced captive condors that had not returned to the nest during their egg's hatching period.)

By the time USFWS personnel could get to the unfortunate nestling, it was dead. Nevertheless, important lessons had been learned. Three condors in California now had experience incubating an egg, and one had experience hatching a nestling. In addition, we learned that trio situations borne of having a tiny population of adults with few choices for mates would not result in successful nestings. Henceforth, trios were broken up by recapturing one bird and holding it until the remaining pair was able to cement its bond enough to resist the intrusions of a third bird.

2002: A Year of Victories and Disappointments

Biologists in Arizona and California looked forward to the onset of the 2002 breeding season. Surely this would be the year that a wild-bred, wild-hatched, wild-raised California condor nestling would fledge. In mid-February 2002, USFWS officials in California announced that they had confirmed their first egg of the year. Reports of two more pairs laying eggs in California soon followed.

The Arizona condors were quick to follow their counterparts in California. Courtship displays that had begun intermittently in October 2001 reached a crescendo in January 2002, with all the breeding-aged condors involved. On January 9, field biologist Kevin Fairhurst, who was stationed in the valley below the Vermilion Cliffs, documented an unprecedented twenty-three courtship displays involving eight different birds. Condor 123, the most dominant condor in the flock, displayed a remarkable eleven times to at least four different females.

By the time the frenzy of the courtship season began to dissipate, we found ourselves with two breeding pairs. The first of these, Condors 123 and 127, had been associating since the failure of the trio's nest attempt the previous year. Although we had initially been saddened that our independent-minded Condor 119 had lost her mate after losing her egg, we

Female Condor 119 (left) and male Condor 122 (right) have delighted tourists at Grand Canyon by repeatedly nesting in a large cave that is visible to the public from viewpoints along the South Rim's Hermit Road. Condor 119 is believed to have produced the first documented condor egg laid in the wild since the inception of the reintroduction program.

did not have long to worry about her single-status. By summer's end she was associating with Condor 122, and the two soon became inseparable.

While the Badger nest cave had been a tremendous start for our inexperienced condors, all four birds set their sights exponentially higher in 2002, selecting spectacular nest sites in cliffs adjacent to Grand Canyon's South Rim. Condors 119 and 122 chose an enormous cave in a butte named The Battleship, beginning incubation at the end of February. Less than a week later, Condors 123 and 127 laid their egg in a smaller cave in nearby Dana Butte. Both nests were at least four hundred feet (122 m) above the ground. To the delight of visitors

to Grand Canyon National Park, both nests could be viewed through spotting scopes from viewpoints along the South Rim's Hermit Road without causing any disturbance to the distant birds. It was a unique situation in which the public and dozens of volunteer nest watchers could witness conservation history in the making.

While we waited impatiently for our eggs to hatch in Arizona, California made an exciting announcement: on April 11, the first of their eggs hatched. Although they had had a nestling hatch from a captive-produced egg in 2001, this was the first hatchling that was produced and hatched in the wild in eighteen years.

More good news was soon to come. Exactly a month later, California's second egg hatched successfully. Then, a few weeks later, at the end of May, their third pair also succeeded in hatching their egg. California condors were finally reproducing in the wild again.

Meanwhile, things were unfolding with a little less drama and a little more disappointment in Arizona. As the expected hatch dates for our condor eggs drew near, our anticipation climbed. Because we could not see into the deep caves our condors had selected, we would have to determine whether our eggs had hatched based on subtle changes in the adults' behavior. They had been averaging two to four days between incubation switches (one bird leaving the nest when the other returned to take over incubation duties); we expected to see them beginning to switch at least daily and possibly more frequently once the egg hatched. As the chick emerges

More good news was soon to come. Exactly a month later, California's second egg hatched successfully.

from the shell, both parents seem to take an avid interest in the newcomer and take their respective turns keeping the youngster warm more frequently than they do their egg. But as carefully as we watched our birds' activities as the projected hatch dates came and went, no noteworthy changes occurred.

Then, on May 3, our hopes soared. Condor 122 relieved 119 at the nest early in the morning and then 119 returned to the cave in the afternoon and took 122's place. It was the first time our birds had had a daily nest switch. But the next morning, both parents spent more than two hours away from the nest, a very long period of time to leave a newly hatched nestling alone. The pair eventually returned to the nest, and 119 disappeared inside. But they left again in the afternoon, and when the pair finally returned, they settled down to roost *outside* the cave. Clearly their nest had failed. Either their egg had been infertile or it had not hatched successfully.

Our hopes turned to Condors 123 and 127. We waited and waited, but witnessed no evidence of a hatching. Another month dragged by, and the pair diligently kept up with their every-two-to-four-day nest switches. Finally, in the final days of May, their dedication to their nest began to wane, and over the next few days their visits petered out altogether. They had incubated for a month longer than should have been necessary before finally giving up on their effort.

In the hopes of learning why our birds had failed to successfully hatch their eggs, Grand Canyon National Park ranger Greg Moore undertook the dangerous task of entering both nests in the weeks following their failures. After a long and arduous hike out to The Battleship, the park climbing crew set up their ropes, and Moore was soon dangling in front of the cave's entrance. To his dismay, however, he discovered that a large overhang prevented him from swinging into the cave. Hanging two hundred feet (60 m) from the cliff rim and four hundred feet (120 m) above the ground, Moore showed his determination and resourcefulness by repeatedly tossing a knotted climbing rope toward a large rock that sat on the nest cave's entrance ledge. After minutes of agonizing effort, Moore finally managed to snag his rope on the rock and pull himself into the cave.

To Moore's amazement, the cave was enormous, perhaps forty feet (12 m) deep and eight to ten feet (2.5–3 m) wide in places. Aside from a small bone that was later confirmed as the remains of a Pleistocene shrub ox, Moore found only condor eggshell fragments, leading us to suspect that the nest had failed during the hatching period.

Unfortunately, an overhanging ledge also stymied Greg's entrance into the Dana Butte cave when he attempted to enter it shortly after it was abandoned by Condors 123 and 127. This time, however, attempts to lodge his knotted rope on a small boulder in the nest entrance resulted in the boulder inching toward him—not a desirable scenario when you're dangling hundreds of feet above the ground. Reluctantly, Moore abandoned his attempt to enter the nest. Nevertheless, as he positioned himself to take photographs of the nest site, he saw a beautiful, white condor egg at the back of the cave, tantalizingly out of reach. Either the egg had been infertile, or it had failed to hatch for some other reason. We would have to wait another year for our birds to try again. Our hopes turned to California, as we avidly followed

Our hopes turned to California, as we avidly followed the news of their rapidly developing chicks.

the news of their rapidly developing chicks. Would a wild-hatched condor soon spread its wings and launch itself from its nest?

Sadly, trouble soon befell the California birds. In mid-September, when California's first chick was five months old (one month before fledging age), its father, Condor 100, disappeared. Despite intensive searches he was never seen again. Because the battery on his transmitter was solar powered, it is quite possible that the solar panel would not have been able to get the necessary light for it to recharge if he died in a crevice or lying on his transmitter. Although Condor 100 had also been wearing a conventional transmitter, its battery had failed only days before, and the USFWS crew had not had an opportunity to trap him to replace it.

Allan Mee, a post-doctoral student working with the condor program for the San Diego Zoological Society, and the USFWS crew overseeing the southern California condor release area continued to monitor Condor 100's chick, hoping that Condor 108 could care for it alone and remaining ready to intervene on the chick's behalf if she could not. Over the next few weeks, Condor 108 seemed to be compensating adequately for her missing mate. On October 2, when the chick was not seen

AC-9's Return to the Wild

AC-9 was the last California condor left in the wild in 1987. With his dramatic capture on Easter Sunday 1987, California was bereft of condors for the first time in thousands of years. To many, the capture of AC-9 meant the end of the California condor. Captive-raised birds, they felt sure, would be an inferior, inadequate substitute. To others, confining AC-9 to a zoo pen was a devastating necessity; to allow him to fly free was to guarantee his and likely his species' demise.

AC-9 spent the next fifteen years in captivity. It is difficult to conceive how a creature that can fly hundreds of miles in a day and that seems to belong to the skies could adjust to life in a flight pen. At least superficially, AC-9 did just that, producing sixteen offspring for the captive-breeding program. In 1992, AC-9's daughter Xewe became the first condor to return to the wild, taking her place in the skies and landscapes that her father had known so intimately. Over the years, more and more of AC-9's progeny flew free, including one son (Condor 122) and one daughter (Condor 149) in Arizona.

After AC-9's former mate, AC-8, returned to the wild successfully, many began to voice the hope that AC-9 might be next. However, unlike AC-8, who no longer appeared to be reproducing, AC-9 was successfully rearing young condors that would be reintroduced to the wild. Setting him free would mean not only losing him from the captive-breeding program but also placing him at risk, because lead poisoning and other threats remained so prevalent in AC-9's former habitat. Should he die in the wild, the California Condor Recovery Program would lose one of its most successful breeders and parents as well as the best-known and most beloved of all condors.

Proponents for setting AC-9 free argued that his genes were well represented both in the wild and in captivity. He might very well take one of the reintroduced condors as a mate and raise young successfully in the wild, teaching a new generation of young condors valuable life lessons.

Ultimately, the arguments for releasing AC-9 won out, and on May 1, 2002, biologists returned AC-9 to the wild amidst tremendous fanfare. An emotional group of supporters watched this historic moment from a distance, eyes filling with tears, and throats choked with emotion. To see the last wild condor flying free once again, something few had dared hope for, let alone expect to witness, was indescribably moving. The California Condor Recovery Program had come full circle.

AC-9 was soon revisiting his old haunts, but it took him longer than expected to become a dominant member of a condor flock, which viewed him as an interloper. By 2004, however, the twenty-four-year-old AC-9 had become more dominant and attracted a young mate, a six-year-old that had been released originally in the Big Sur area of central California. To everyone's delight, the pair selected a remote cave in the Sespe Condor Sanctuary, and the young female laid an egg, which the pair immediately began incubating.

On Easter Sunday, April 11, 2004, seventeen years after AC-9 was brought into captivity, AC-9's chick emerged from its egg and greeted the wilderness to which his father had so recently been returned.

The last of the wild California condors to be taken into captivity in 1987, twenty-two-year-old AC-9 returns to the wild on May 1, 2002. Despite having spent fifteen years in captivity, AC-9 adapted quickly to life in the wild: by 2004 he had found a mate, and he subsequently raised a chick with her.

in the cave entrance, biologists optimistically thought it had fledged. Field biologists were unable to locate it from their distant viewing point over the next two days. Accordingly, on October 4, then USFWS Deputy Condor Project Leader Greg Austin hiked in to the nest area for a closer look. Sadly, upon reaching the nest cliff, he reported seeing a pile of feathers on a ledge below the cave. "Then I saw the flies," he said, "and I knew it was too late."

Unfortunately, the chick was partially decomposed, and necropsy results were inconclusive. Nevertheless, some suspected that lead poisoning might have been a contributing factor. Both parents had been foraging for natural food as well as taking advantage of calf carcasses supplied to them by the USFWS field crew, and upon being trapped, female Condor 108 was found to have elevated lead levels.

On October 2, when the chick was not seen in the cave entrance, biologists optimistically thought it had fledged.

If the parent condors did indeed feed on a carcass containing lead, they could have regurgitated tainted meat to their hapless offspring.

Only two weeks later, Mee failed to spot the second California chick in its cave entrance. His first thought was that it had fledged. As he watched the empty cave entrance, however, he saw male Condor 98, who had been an exceptionally attentive parent, move out of the shadows dragging his dead chick. The necropsy that was performed as soon as the chick's body was recovered provided astonishing information. Radiographs revealed that the chick's digestive tract was clogged by no fewer than twelve bottle caps, shards of glass and plastic, electrical fixtures, screws, and washers. The extreme levels of trash in the condor nestling's digestive tract had led either directly or indirectly to its premature death.

All involved in the condor reintroduction program reeled with shock upon looking at the X-rays and the photos of the chick's stomach contents. What had seemed like a harmless activity when we watched adult condors play with trash suddenly made its desperately serious consequences apparent as we realized that they might subsequently regurgitate that trash into the mouth of a nestling. Although adult condors periodically cast pellets that might rid their own systems of trash (no trash has been seen in a radiograph of an adult condor), nestling condors typically do not regurgitate pellets unless they go hungry for extended periods of time. As a result, they likely have limited mechanisms by which to rid themselves of any trash fed to them by their unwitting parents.

Dismayed by the loss of the first two chicks, researchers now pinned their hopes on the youngest of the California nestlings. I cannot imagine Mee's devastation on October 21 when he watched male Condor 107 drag *its* dead chick into view from the back of its cave in a remote portion of the Los

Padres National Forest. The unimaginable had happened: all three chicks had perished. The day after discovering the third dead chick, Mee looked on sadly as its father, Condor 107, aggressively defended the body of his chick against the two-legged intruders who had come to take it away.

Although some trash was found in the third chick's nest, X-rays revealed no trash in the chick's digestive tract, and the cause of death remained uncertain.

Arizona's First Condor Chick

The 2003 condor breeding season started on a high note with at least four eggs being laid, three in Arizona and one in California. In the hopes of preventing the tragedies that had beset the program in California in 2002, the USFWS field crew increased the number of carcasses they provided to their condor flock in case hunger had driven the adults to collect and feed trash to their offspring. In addition, they scattered the feeding area with small bone chips in case the condors were picking up bits of trash that to them resembled bone fragments to supplement a possible lack of calcium in their diets.

In an even more proactive bid to avoid the repetition of a nestling dying from ingesting trash, personnel in California climbed into the nest during the egg stage and sifted the cave substrate to remove any trash that might be available to the adults or their future offspring. They found a bottle cap packed with glass shards and calf hair, as well as the wadding from a shotgun shell that was also mixed with calf hair. Although some had thought that the trash found in nests in California might have been placed there by ravens, which are renowned for caching interesting objects, the presence of calf hair mixed in with the garbage was evidence that adult condors had ingested the trash, because they often cast pellets composed of calf hair after feeding on their supplemental carcasses.

While a new pair tried nesting in California, both the Arizona pairs whose nests attempts had failed in 2002 tried again in the spring of 2003. In addition, four condors attempted nesting for the first time in a cave in the Vermilion Cliffs. Unfortunately, the foursome did not consist of two separate pairs laying eggs in two nest caves, but rather of a quad of two males and two females that continuously associated with each other and settled together on one nest cave. Knowing that trios didn't work, we could not help but feel that a quad would be equally ineffective. But in late February, before we could determine which birds to trap to break up the quad, one of the condors laid an egg, and all four subsequently took turns with incubation duties. Unfortunately, the cave was narrow, and either the traffic of four birds in and out of the nest or competition over incubation duties led to the egg being broken within a week of its having been laid.

By early March, based on their behavior, we knew that both our condor pairs had laid their respective eggs. Condors 119 and 122 were once again using their Battleship nest cave. Condors 123 and 127, on the other hand, had moved westward to the Salt Creek drainage and selected a new cave that was not visible from the South Rim. The exact nest location could only be confirmed by undertaking a grueling twenty-four-mile (39-km) round-trip hike into the canyon.

Grand Canyon National Park's condor biologist, Chad Olson, who oversaw the condors' nesting activities in the park, made the first of what would be countless treks into Salt Creek on March 14, 2003. With surprising ease given the immensity of the canyon and the countless caves that penetrated its innumerable cliffs, Olson quickly determined which cave the pair was using and confirmed, based on the adults' behavior, that they were indeed incubating.

Like the Battleship and Dana Butte caves, the Salt Creek cave was too deep to allow a clear view

Anxiously we watched our condors' behavior hoping for a change that would indicate they finally had a nestling.

into the nest. Over the next few months, the extraordinarily hot spring and summer temperatures and the lack of water in the Salt Creek drainage hampered our efforts to observe the birds' activities from within the canyon. Instead, we had to satisfy ourselves with determining how their nesting was progressing from

the canyon rim based on their comings and goings and the blips emitted by their radio transmitters.

California's egg hatched in the second week of May. Anxiously we watched our condors' behavior hoping for a change that would indicate they finally had a nestling. To our dismay, though, in a repeat of 2002's patterns, around the time their egg should have hatched, Condors 119 and 122 began spending more and more time together out of their nest and finally stopped returning to it altogether. Last year's nest failures had been expected. Inexperienced condors often take a year or two before they can successfully hatch an egg. But this year's disappointment cut deep. We had waited so long for our birds to grow up, and now we would have to wait yet another year for this pair to try again.

A few days after the pair abandoned their Battleship nest, we once again sought answers for the failure. This time, we also hoped to get more detailed information about the nest contents and sift for trash if necessary. Accordingly, Grand Canyon National Park's helicopter deposited Olson, who would conduct the biological work on the top of The Battleship along with rangers Greg Moore and Brenton White, and left them to begin the daring and arduous task of getting into the enormous nest cave. With White belaying them from above, Moore and Olson cautiously rappelled down to the cave. From our vantage point on the rim about a mile away, the two climbers, visible only through binoculars, looked like spiderlings drifting on tenuous threads over the immense space of the canyon. Soon they disappeared inside the black hole of the cave, and we waited tensely to hear what they would find.

After what seemed like an eternity, Olson's voice, laced with disappointment, crackled over the radio: "Well, we found eggshell fragments again."

Like the previous year, it appeared that the birds' nesting attempt had failed during the hatching stage. Perhaps the embryo had been malpositioned (prior to hatching, the chick must be positioned with its head tucked under its right wing and its bill pointed toward the air cell at the large end of the egg so that the chick can breathe when it breaks through the egg's internal membrane before breaking through the external shell). Maybe the chick had been unable to extricate itself from the shell. Perhaps the parents had fought over the egg and accidentally broken it. We could only speculate on what had happened.

Olson continued, "There is some trash in here. Not too much, but a couple of bottle tops, some cloth . . ."

Many had hoped that having condors nest in a national park as outwardly pristine as Grand Canyon would make them immune to the trash problem experienced in California. Having seen the plastic bottle tops, hats, and plastic wrappers that littered the cliffs below Grand Canyon Village, however, we had had concerns that Arizona's condors would also consume garbage and feed it to their chicks.

Our disappointment about the broken eggshell and the presence of trash in the Battleship nest later was alleviated by a very special discovery. Olson found more than just eggshell fragments and trash in

Soon they disappeared inside the black hole of the cave, and we waited tensely to hear what they would find.

the condors' nest cave. Sifting the powdery substance at the back of the cave, he had found large bones. Old bones. Subsequent analysis by paleontological expert Jim Mead of Northern Arizona University revealed that they were the bones of Pleistocene adult and juvenile California condors. Our captive-raised condors may not have hatched their egg this year, but, remarkably, they had chosen a nest used by their ancestors thousands of years earlier.

Now it was time to put our disappointment in 119 and 122's nest failure behind us and focus on Condors 123 and 127. Perhaps they too could follow in their ancestor's footsteps and produce a nestling high in a cliff in the Grand Canyon. When 123 and 127 started switching nest duties on a daily basis, we could scarcely believe that they might actually have hatched their egg. Most likely they would go back to switching nest duties every three to four days and would then abandon their nest. But after three weeks of monitoring consistent nest exchanges, our early caution tumbled headlong into euphoria. Arizona had its first modern-day condor chick.

As the summer progressed, Condors 123 and 127 appeared to be on constant food-finding missions. At the age of one month, a condor nestling can thermoregulate (maintain its body temperature) on its own and no longer needs to be brooded by its

Cost
of the
Reintroduction
Program

The California Condor Recovery Program is frequently touted as the costliest program to restore an endangered species of all time. Because California condors are long-lived, slow-reproducing creatures, the species' recovery is a lengthy process. The estimated cost currently mentioned in the press is about $35 million. While $35 million sounds like a large sum, efforts to bring back condors have been underway for close to three decades, amounting to a relatively small per-year expenditure. The $30–40 million (excluding security costs) spent on President George W. Bush's second inaugural celebration, the $850 million it cost to put two rovers on Mars, the greater than $10 million yearly salaries of numerous baseball players, all help put expenditures for saving condors in perspective. In 2004 a Picasso painting sold at auction for more than $104 million, and Vincent Van Gogh's "Irises" sold for $49 million in 1987, the year the last wild condor was taken into captivity. Can a species as uniquely magnificent as the California condor truly be worth less to us than one painting?

Much of what is spent on condors comes from private donations, not federal sources. Less than half the Peregrine Fund's yearly budget for captive-rearing condors and reintroducing them in Arizona comes from the USFWS, and the remainder comes from private sources. The yearly cost of recovering condors in Arizona is roughly equivalent to fighting one moderate-sized wildfire on the Kaibab Plateau.

Much of the money spent on the condor program has gone toward buying land and protecting habitat, expenditures that benefit a host of species. Moreover, as a flagship endangered species, the condor has focused a positive spotlight on the Endangered Species Act and has elicited support for other endangered organisms. Condor recovery is by no means assured. Nevertheless, tremendous progress has been made. Where once only twenty-two condors remained in existence, the population approaches three hundred today. Should condor recovery ultimately succeed and condors be taken off the endangered species list, the effort will represent one of the greatest conservation victories of all time, eclipsing the return of the bald eagle, the peregrine falcon, and the gray wolf. Such success would provide many with the hope that we can rectify our earlier short-sightedness, can spare at least a few creatures from human-caused extinctions, and can maintain the splendors of our past for the enjoyment of future generations.

Condors, including wild-hatched Condor 242 (upper right), loaf on a pinnacle at day's end. A supreme effort by committed individuals has saved the California condor from extinction. Whether future generations will see condors flying over the canyons of the Southwest will depend on the continued willingness of the public to address the remaining threats in the condor's range.

parents to stay warm. Accordingly, the parents spend increasing time away from the nest searching for the endless food their chick needs to fuel its spectacular growth. Condors cannot carry anything in their feet and do not do so in their bills. Instead, they ingest food, hold it in their crops, and regurgitate it into their chick's awaiting mouth upon returning to the nest. The young Arizona parents fed their chick a smorgasbord of food consisting of meat from mule deer, elk, a mule, several unidentified carcasses, and the occasional remains of calf carcasses put out for them at the release site. On one extraordinary occasion, Condor 123 left the nest area, flew fifty-four miles (86 km) north to the release site, fed himself, returned to the nest area, fed the chick, then returned to the release area where he roosted. He then returned to the chick with a cropful of food first thing the following morning, having traveled more than two hundred

On one occasion, biologists watched the pair chase a golden eagle from the vicinity of their nest. ∼

miles (320 km), flying almost constantly during daylight hours to ferry food back and forth to his hungry nestling.

In California, where field personnel could observe the activities inside their nest with relative ease, the condor parents showed that the quality of their care extended beyond the time they spent preening and cuddling up to their nestling, and the tireless foraging trips made to sustain it. On one occasion, biologists watched the pair chase a golden eagle from the vicinity of their nest. On another day, the parents united to drive off a black bear that had managed to get within twenty feet (6 m) of their somewhat-accessible nest entrance. Clearly, although the quality of their habitat might conspire against their ability to raise a chick successfully, the condors in California and Arizona were showing themselves to be exemplary parents.

Condor 305: Success at Last

With the coming of the monsoon rains and the slightly cooler temperatures that accompanied them, we decided that a trek into the canyon to get a visual confirmation of the Arizona chick was long overdue. Although 123 and 127's behavior had left no doubt in our minds that they were caring for a nestling, two volunteer nest watchers who had made the only condor-viewing trip into the scorching Salt Creek drainage had not seen the chick. Until we were able to confirm the chick visually, some members of the press, the public, and even the condor program remained unconvinced of the chick's existence. To avoid the still-extraordinary daytime heat, Chad Olson and I resolved to make the long hike into the canyon at night. To our surprise, as we drove to the trailhead on the evening of August 15, we were treated not to the stultifying heat we had expected, but to rain, hail, and unusually chilly temperatures. Fortunately, the skies began to clear after our first hour of hiking.

We carried several days' worth of water and food, binoculars, a spotting scope, a tripod, radiotelemetry equipment, a tent, sleeping bags, and personal gear. Despite the load, we quickly discovered that the Grand Canyon is a magical place at night. Devoid of people, the canyon embraced us in velvety darkness. The deep shadows of tall cliffs loomed around us; a tapestry of stars sparkled above. We walked to the musical accompaniment of feeding bats, dodged the occasional scorpion, and relished the peaceful stillness and the cool air. It was a hike we would repeat over and over in the months to come.

We set up camp at 1:00 AM and roused ourselves a few hours later to hike the steep slope from camp to our chosen viewing area. Dawn splashed across the sky, setting the canyon's cliffs aglow. The narrow Salt Creek drainage, though, remained in shadow, its magnificent red cliffs evoking the area's other designated name: The Inferno. We reached our viewing spot, and Olson, who still was one of only three people who knew which cave was the nest, eagerly sought the cave entrance with binoculars. Seconds later, without saying a word, he lowered them and speedily set up the spotting scope.

"Have a look," he offered, a smile breaking across his face as he allowed me the first close-up, spotting-scope view of what he had glimpsed in the cave's black entrance: a condor chick. Arizona's *first* documented condor chick. I gazed at the magnificent sight.

The condor chick appeared to be in wonderful health. We watched the **nestling preen,** *stretch, and flap his wings.* ⌒

The surprisingly large, full-grown, black-feathered, black-headed vulture filling the circular view in my spotting scope was not quite four months old. The condor chick appeared to be in wonderful health. We watched the nestling preen, stretch, and flap his wings. A large butterfly and later a flying turkey vulture caught his eye, and he cocked his head, eyes alight with curiosity, as he watched them pass by. The following day, we watched a speck on the horizon turn into Condor 127 as she hurtled toward the cave to feed her youngster. Reluctantly, we finally tore ourselves away. Leaving behind the peace and otherworldliness of the canyon and the timelessness we had experienced while observing a few days in a young condor's life, we ascended into a chaos of media and publicity.

Several days later, our nestling received his name: Condor 305. From that point on, there were endless trips into the canyon by Peregrine Fund and Grand Canyon National Park personnel. Typically we hiked in at night, spent three or four days camped out in the Salt Creek drainage watching 305, and hiked out again on the night of our last day. From September on, every waking moment of Condor 305's life would be watched and monitored.

We could leave nothing to chance. Although his fate would ultimately lie beyond our control, we would be present to assist in any way we could should the need arise. We would document his feedings, his activity levels, his health, and ultimately, if all went as hoped, his first flight from his natal cave.

Meanwhile, in California, the nestling that had been dubbed Condor 308 appeared to be progressing as well as Arizona's Condor 305. To give their chick every chance at success, California field personnel decided to climb into the nest to remove any potential trash, give the chick a health check and a vaccination against West Nile Virus, and outfit it with tags and transmitters so it could be monitored from the moment it left the nest. Mike Clark, the head condor zookeeper from the Los Angeles Zoo, entered the nest and captured Condor 308 without incident. But then, as the attendant veterinarian began 308's health check, all appearances of normalcy began to unravel.

Condor 308 had looked fine through the distant lens of a spotting scope, although Condor Recovery Team Leader Mike Wallace and Clark had commented to each other that he looked more like a three-month-old than a four-month-old chick. In the hand, though, the team discovered with a shock that Condor 308, who by now should have had ten-to-twelve-inch-long (25–30-cm-long) tail feathers, had no tail at all. His flight feathers were poorly developed, and he was underweight. The chick was feisty and appeared to behave normally, but a disturbing rasping noise accompanied his breathing. A palpitation of the nestling's crop revealed a number of hard

objects that could have been but did not feel like bone. Perhaps a blockage had affected the bird's nutrition and stunted its growth. Reluctantly, the team decided to return with a helicopter to transport the nestling to the Los Angeles Zoo for X-rays and a more thorough examination.

Less than forty-eight hours later, field personnel flushed Condor 308's parents away from the nest so they would not see their chick's removal and would remain at the nest cave, thinking their chick was still present, over the few hours that the team expected it to be absent. Prior to transport, the chick was given oxygen, wrapped in a black cloth to ease his fears about the goings-on around him, and draped in icy towels to keep him cool. At the zoo the chick was given supportive fluids, antibiotics, and a full exam by Los Angeles Zoo veterinarian Dr. Cynthia Stringfield. Inconclusive X-rays and the continued raspy breathing, however, convinced the veterinary staff to hold the chick overnight so they could conduct a still more intensive investigation.

By early the following morning the chick had regurgitated most of its crop contents in a fairly typical stress response. To the team's dismay, the crop contents included a portion of a plastic shotgun shell, four aluminum pop-top rings, a bottle cap, several pieces of glass, two pieces of rubber, an electrical connector, two pieces of bark, and three pieces of melted metal. Given the chick's poor nutritional status, its raspy breathing, its compromised condition, and the likelihood that more trash was present farther down its digestive tract, the difficult decision was made to keep the chick in captivity and work to restore its good health. Surgery revealed further bad news: one of the objects ingested by the chick had punctured its digestive and respiratory tracts. The doomed nestling could not be saved. California's hope for a wild fledgling was euthanized on the operating table.

When we received the devastating news from California, my unshakable faith that the condors were going to make it faltered for the first time. If our environment was so contaminated that condors could not reproduce successfully in the wild despite their best efforts, then all our releases of captive-raised condors would ultimately be for naught. The California condor would either remain in zoos or slip once and for all over the threshold of extinction.

California had had four chicks over the last two years. None had survived. As I watched Condor 305 flapping his wings, running into the back of his cave then bouncing back into view and hopping up onto the entrance rock at the front of his cave, I dared not hope that his chances were any better. But looking at 305—at his long tail, sleek flight feathers, bright eyes, and energetic demeanor—it was hard to imagine that his condition might be compromised by having ingested trash or lead bullet fragments (although hunting season was underway on the Kaibab Plateau). He radiated energy, health, and curiosity.

And with the passing of each fall day, he increasingly scared us to death. As he approached fledging age, Condor 305 took to clambering out onto what looked like an inch-wide ledge that stretched out from the west side of his cave. Toes

clinging to the ledge, body pressed up against the cliff face, he would try to beat his enormous wings against the rock wall. Would he fall the four hundred feet (120 m) to the ground before he was ready to fledge? Invariably, though, he would wrench himself back into the cave from the precarious ledge, and we would breathe a sigh of relief. Each day, 305's bouts of activity—mad-flapping and sprinting around the cave like a crazed rabbit—increased in frequency.

Each two-person team watching the nest cave hoped that they would be the ones to see 305 take his first leap into the sky. Each team packed up reluctantly when their stint in the canyon came to an end. Fears lingered. Three of California's chicks had made it to within a few weeks of fledging before they had died. Would 305 be any different?

Late on the night of November 3, I hiked in to Salt Creek to join Olson for yet another stint of nest watching. On my second day in the canyon, November 5, Condor 305 appeared to have given up on the idea of leaping out of his cave. Unusually quiet, his first bout of activity did not begin until 1:15 PM (a time when he was usually on his second or third). Fighting against the tranquilizing boredom of watching a bird doze in its nest entrance for hours on end, we struggled to stay focused.

Finally, 305 began a typical bout of flapping and running around and trying to clamber out of the cave. As though to make up for his morning of inactivity, his afternoon energy bout went on a bit longer than usual. Just as it seemed like he was finally winding down, at 1:39 PM, 305 craned his neck, looked fixedly at an imaginary ledge, and leaped toward it. Olson and I shot to our feet. "He's fledging! He's fledging!" we yelled to each other— and then watched in horror as 305 plummeted earthward. Instead of the horizontal flight we'd expected, he was in freefall. Wings half outstretched, he fell like a maple seed buffeted by a fall wind: two hundred feet, three hundred feet. Microseconds elapsed, but it felt like an eternity. Finally, astonishingly gently given his near-vertical descent, 305 touched down at the base of the cliff, directly below his nest cave. He didn't move. We didn't move. Minutes passed. And then, Condor 305 did what any self-respecting young condor would do: reaching over to a banana yucca a few inches away, he opened his bill, clamped on, and gave it several sharp tugs. Olson and I burst out laughing. Our young condor was just fine. Condor 305 had begun

Finally, 305 began a typical bout of flapping and running around and trying to clamber out of the cave.

to explore the new elements of his world the way all condors do, by investigating them with his bill, tugging, pulling, and feeling things out.

An hour later, Condor 127 flew over Salt Creek. She and her mate had been absent for three days, in search of carcasses to feed their hungry chick.

Landing at her nest, she walked back into its dark interior to feed her nestling. But he was gone. She came out to the entrance and looked around. Far below the nest, she spotted what looked like her chick madly flopping his wings around in the universal way that young birds solicit food from parents. (Although common to all birds, this wing-begging or food-begging behavior looks quite a bit more dramatic in a bird with a nine-foot wingspan than it does in a small sparrow!) Despite the chick's frenzied activity on the ground far below the nest, Condor 127 went in and out of the nest several times, perhaps to reassure herself that her chick was not tucked into a corner of the cave. Then, flying down to the ground, she fed Condor 305 his first meal as a free-flying condor.

Many months of clambering onto cliff ledges and short, hesitant flights passed before Condor 305 finally soared out of the Salt Creek drainage. In the spring of 2004, as condors once again began to nest in Arizona and California, 305 treated thousands of visitors at the South Rim to the sight of a wild-hatched condor flying free, with no transmitters or numbered wing tags, offering a glimpse of what once had been, a glimpse of the future still to come.

Recent Failings and Fledgings

California finally fledged a chick successfully in the fall of 2004. Prior to that, however, they lost one more chick to trash ingestion and had a second chick (the first of AC-9's chicks since his re-release to the wild) fall from the nest and break a wing at the age of about four months. AC-9's chick underwent surgery to remove trash that he too had ingested and to fix his wing. Thanks to the Los Angeles Zoo staff's efforts (including twice-daily physical therapy on the recovering wing), the condor will fly free one day. Sadly, in 2005, one of California's latest two chicks had to be removed from its nest and undergo surgery to remove ingested trash that was compromising its development. California's second 2005 chick succumbed to West Nile Virus—the first California condor to do so. As of the end of 2005, the situation for condors in California remained dire; only one chick had fledged successfully in the wild out of nine nestlings and at least five chicks had either died or been compromised by trash ingestion. The best course of action to enable condors in California to reproduce successfully (such as encouraging them to forage more naturally, the way the Arizona condors do) is still being debated.

In 2004 in Arizona, Condors 119 and 122 finally hatched their first chick, to the delight of thousands of tourists and dozens of nest-watch volunteers who could observe the activities of the young chick and its parents from a distant viewpoint along Hermit Road. This time, Olson watched the graceful fledging we had always envisioned, when 119 and 122's chick, Condor 350, launched expertly

from his Battleship nest on Thanksgiving Day 2004 and glided gracefully to the ground.[II]

Arizona Condors 114 and 149 also nested successfully in 2004 and fledged a chick from a cave in the Vermilion Cliffs. The following spring, 149 abandoned her homebody mate and returned to her haunts at the South Rim. Condor 114, meanwhile, finally accepted the mate I had always been convinced would be perfect for him, the second biggest homebody in the Arizona condor flock, Condor 126. Nesting in the same cave he had used the year before with 149, Condor 114 raised a chick for the second year in succession, a feat no doubt facilitated by the readily available food at the release site less than a mile away.

Also in 2005, Condors 123 and 127, Condor 305's parents, laid another egg in their Salt Creek nest cave and undertook the intensive task of raising and fledging their second nestling.

With several successful condor fledgings in Arizona, it now seems likely that each year, more and more wild-raised juvenile condors will thrill visitors as they drift with effortless grace over the Grand Canyon, free, for a time, of tags and transmitters. All eventually will be captured and outfitted with identifying number tags and a means to

---

[II] *In 2006, Condors 119 and 122's attempt to hatch another egg failed during the incubation stage because field biologists recaptured 122 due to acute lead poisoning. He spent nearly a year in captivity undergoing treatment and recovering. Condor 119 was unable to incubate alone and ultimately abandoned the egg.*

Unaware of his renown as the first condor chick to fledge in the wild in twenty-one years, Condor 305 thrills visitors to Grand Canyon National Park as he flies over the South Rim. Very few of the people who saw 305 had ever seen a condor without wing tag numbers and transmitters.

After several unsuccessful attempts at hatching a chick, Condors 119 and 122 successfully raised Condor 350 (left), which fledged November 25, 2004. Juvenile condors have already attained their nine-foot wingspan upon leaving their nest caves for the first time at the age of about six months.

track them. Condors' numbers are still too few to leave their future to chance. But I now feel sure that the day will come when California condors will fly into the future unfettered by the trappings that symbolize our desperate attempts to right the wrongs we have inflicted on them. They will fly free, as they once did, fresh wind whistling through their unadorned wings, vast landscapes unfurling beneath their ever-curious, somehow all-knowing gaze.

Austin, William, Shawn Farry, Bill Heinrich, Jeff Humphrey, Elaine Leslie, Susan MacVean, Chad Olson, Sophie Osborn, Bruce Palmer, Chris Parish, and Michael Small. *A Review of the First Five Years of the California Condor Reintroduction Program in Northern Arizona.* Sacramento, Calif.: U.S. Fish and Wildlife Service, California/Nevada Operations Office, 2002.

Brown, Herbert. "The California Vulture in Arizona." *Auk* 16 (1899): 272.

Cade, Tom J., Sophie A. H. Osborn, W. Grainger Hunt, and Christopher P. Woods. "Commentary on released California condors *Gymnogyps californianus* in Arizona." In *Raptors Worldwide*, edited by Robin D. Chancellor and Bernd U. Meyberg, 11–25. Budapest, Hungary: World Working Group on Birds of Prey and Owls/MME-Birdlife Hungary, 2004.

Chemnick, Leona G., Arlene T. Kumamoto, and Oliver A. Ryder. "Genetic Analyses in Support of Conservation Efforts for the California Condor." *International Zoo Yearbook* 37 (2000): 330–339.

Clark, Robert G., and Robert D. Ohmart. "Spread-Winged Posture of Turkey Vultures: Single or Multiple Function? *Condor* 87 (1985): 350–355.

Cohn, Jeffrey P. "Saving the California Condor." *BioScience* 49, no. 11 (1999): 864–868.

Collins, Paul W., Noel F. R. Snyder, and Steven D. Emslie. "Faunal Remains in California Condor Nest Caves." *Condor* 102 (2000): 222–227.

Coues, Elliott. "Life of the Birds of Fort Whipple, Arizona: With Which Are Incorporated All other Species to Inhabit the Territory; with Brief Critical and Field Notes, Descriptions of New Species, etc." *Proceedings of the Academy of Natural Sciences of Philadelphia* 18 (1866): 39–100.

DeSaussure, Raymond. "Remains of the California Condor in Arizona Caves." *Plateau* 29 (1956): 44–45.

Eisler, Ronald. "Lead Hazards to Fish, Wildlife, and Invertebrates: A Synoptic Review." U.S. Fish and Wildlife Service Biological Report 85(1.14), 1988.

Emslie, Steven. D. "Canyon Echoes of the Condor." *Natural History* 4 (1986): 10–14.

———. "Age and Diet of Fossil California Condors in Grand Canyon, Arizona." *Science* 237 (1987): 768–770.

———. "The Fossil History and Phylogenetic Relationships of Condors (Ciconiiformes: Vulturidae) in the New World." *Journal of Vertebrate Paleontology* 8 (1988): 212–228.

Finley, William L. "Life History of the California Condor, Part III: Home Life of the Condors." *Condor* 10, no. 2 (1908): 58–65.

Fry, D. Michael. "Assessment of Lead Contamination Sources Exposing California Condors." Final report submitted to California Department of Fish and Game, Sacramento, Calif., 2003. http://www.dfg.ca.gov/hcpb/info/bm_research/bm_pdfrpts/2003_02.pdf (accessed July 5, 2006).

Geyer, Charles J., Oliver A. Ryder, Leona G. Chemnick, and Elizabeth A. Thompson. "Analysis of Relatedness in the California Condors, from DNA Fingerprints." *Molecular Biology and Evolution* 10, no. 3 (1993): 571–589.

Del Hoyo, Joseph, Andrew Elliott, and Jordi Sargatal (eds.). *Handbook of the Birds of the World: New World Vultures to Guineafowl* (vol. 2). Barcelona, Spain: Lynx Edicions, 1994.

Harris, Harry. "The Annals of *Gymnogyps* to 1900." *Condor* 43 (1941): 3–55.

Harrison, Ed, and Lloyd F. Kiff. "Apparent Replacement Clutch Laid by Wild California Condor." *Condor* 82 (1980): 351–352.

Heinrich, Bernd. "An Experimental Investigation of Insight in Common Ravens (*Corvus corax*)." *Auk* 112 (1995): 994–1003.

Houston, David C. "A Possible Function of Sunning Behavior by Griffon Vultures, *Gyps* spp., and Other Large Soaring Birds." *Ibis* 122 (1980): 366–369.

Hunt, W. Grainger, William Burnham, Chris Parish, Kurt Burnham, Brian Mutch, and J. Lindsay Oaks. "Bullet Fragments in Deer Remains: Implications for Lead Exposure in Avian Scavengers." *Wildlife Society Bulletin* 34, no. 1 (2006): 167–170.

Johnson, Terry B., and Barbara A. Garrison. "California Condor Reintroduction Proposal for the Vermilion Cliffs, Northern Arizona." Technical Report 86. Phoenix: Arizona Game and Fish Department, Nongame Endangered Wildlife Program, 1996.

Koford, Carl B. *The California Condor.* Washington, D.C.: National Audubon Society, 1953.

Ligon, J. David. "Relationships of the Cathartid Vultures." *Occasional Papers of the Museum of Zoology University of Michigan* 651 (1967): 1–26.

Lucas, Frederic A. "Animals Recently Extinct or Threatened with Extermination, as Represented in the Collections of the U.S. National Museum. *Report of National Museum* 1889:609–649.

Mead, Jim I. "The Last 30,000 Years of Faunal History within the Grand Canyon, Arizona." *Quaternary Research* 15 (1981): 311–326.

Mead, Jim I., and Arthur M. Philips III. "The Late Pleistocene and Holocene Fauna and Flora of Vulture Cave, Grand Canyon, Arizona." *Southwestern Naturalist* 26, no. 3 (1981): 257–288.

McFarland, David, ed. *The Oxford Companion to Animal Behavior.* Oxford, United Kingdom: Oxford University Press, 1987.

Meretsky, Vicky J., Noel F. R. Snyder, Steven R. Beissinger, David A. Clendenen, and James W. Wiley. "Demography of the California Condor: Implications for Reestablishment." *Conservation Biology* 14, no. 4(2000): 957–967.

Miller, Loye H. "Succession in the Cathartine Dynasty." *Condor* 44 (1942): 212–213.

———. Condor remains from Rampart Cave, Arizona. *Condor* 62 (1960): 70.

Nelson, Lisa. *Ice Age Mammals of the Colorado Plateau.* Flagstaff: Northern Arizona University, 1990.

Osborn, Sophie A. H., and Chad V. Olson. Foraging on Non-Proffered Carcasses by California Condors (*Gymnogyps californianus*) Reintroduced in Northern Arizona. Working Paper, Author's Collection, 2005.

Parmalee, Paul W. "California Condor and Other Birds from Stanton Cave, Arizona." *Journal of the Arizona Academy of Science* 5 (1969): 204–206.

Pattee, Oliver H., Peter H. Bloom, J. Michael Scott, and Milton R. Smith. "Lead Hazards within the Range of the California Condor." *Condor* 92 (1990): 931–937.

Peregrine Fund. Notes from the Field, California Condor Releases in Arizona.

Multiple entries from 1996 to 2005 consulted. http://www.peregrinefund.org/field_notes.asp.

Phillips, Allan, Joe Marshall, and Gale Monson. *The Birds of Arizona.* Tucson: Univ. of Arizona Press, 1964.

Proctor, Noble S., and Patrick J. Lynch. *Manual of Ornithology—Avian Structure and Function.* New Haven, Conn.: Yale Univ. Press, 1993.

Rea, Amadeo M. "California Condor Captive Breeding: A Recovery Proposal." *Environment Southwest* 484 (1981): 8–12.

———. 1983. "Cathartid Affinities: A Brief Overview." In *Vulture Biology and Management*, edited by Sanford R. Wilbur and Jerome A. Jackson. Berkeley: Univ. of California Press, 26–54.

Rhoads, Samuel N. "The Birds of Southeastern Texas and Southern Arizona Observed during May, June, and July 1891." *Proceedings of the Academy of Natural Sciences of Philadelphia* 44 (1892): 114–115.

Sibley, Charles G., and John E. Ahlquist. *Phylogeny and Classification of Birds.* New Haven, Conn.: Yale Univ. Press, 1990.

Sibley, David A. *The Sibley Guide to Birds.* New York: Alfred A. Knopf, 2000.

Snyder, Noel F. R., and Janet A. Hamber. "Replacement-Clutching and Annual Nesting of California Condors." *Condor* 87 (1985): 374–378.

Snyder, Noel F. R., and Amadeo Rea. "California Condor." In *The Raptors of Arizona*, edited by Richard L. Glinski. Tucson: Univ. of Arizona Press, 1998, 32–36.

Snyder, Noel F. R., and N. John Schmitt. 2002. "California Condor (*Gymnogyps californianus*)." In *The Birds of North America*, no. 610, edited by Alan Poole and Frank Gill. Philadelphia: The Birds

of North America, 2002.

Snyder, Noel F. R., and Helen Snyder. "Biology and Conservation of the California Condor." *Current Ornithology* 6 (1989): 175–267.

———. *The California Condor: A Saga of Natural History and Conservation.* London: Academic Press, 2000.

———. *Introduction to the California Condor.* Berkeley: Univ. of California Press, 2005.

Steadman, David W., and Norton G. Miller. "California Condor Associated with Spruce-Jack Pine Woodland in the Late Pleistocene of New York." *Quaternary Research* 28 (1987): 415–426.

Terres, John K. *The Audubon Society Encyclopedia of North American Birds.* New York: Wings Books, 1996.

Thelander, Carl G., and Margo Crabtree, eds. *Life on the Edge: A Guide to California's Endangered Natural Resources: Wildlife.* Santa Cruz, Calif.: BioSystems Books, 1994.

Wetmore, Alexander, and Herbert Friedmann. "The California Condor in Texas." *Condor* 35 (1933): 37–38.

Zoological Society of San Diego. "California's Year of the Condor." *Zoonooz* 56, no. 5 (1983): 4–11.

Front cover, © Christie Van Cleve

Pages ii–iii, © Art Wolfe, Inc.

Page vii, © Don Singer

Opposite page 1, © Elena Miras

Page 5, © Elena Miras

Page 6, © Christie Van Cleve

Page 9, © Ronald S. Phillips/EcoStock

Page 11, © Don Singer

Page 12, © Christie Van Cleve

Page 16, © Christie Van Cleve

Page 17, © Christie Van Cleve

Page 18, top left, © Christie Van Cleve

Page 18, top right, © Christie Van Cleve

Page 18, bottom left, © Christie Van Cleve

Page 18, bottom right, © Christie Van Cleve

Page 20, © Don Singer

Page 23, Courtesy of Steven Emslie

Page 24, Courtesy of the American
Philosophical Society

Page 29, © Christie Van Cleve

Page 35, © Christie Van Cleve

Page 36, Photograph by Phil Ensley; courtesy
of Jan Hamber

Page 37, Photograph by John McNeely;
courtesy of Jan Hamber

Page 39, © François Gohier

Page 42, © Joel Sartore/www.joelsartore.com

Page 44, © Art Wolfe, Inc.

Page 47, © Rankin Harvey/Houserstock

Page 51, © Glenn Oakley

Page 53, Photograph by Chad Olson; courtesy
of the National Park Service

Page 57, Courtesy of the author

Page 58, © Elena Miras

Page 61, © Christie Van Cleve

Page 62, © Christie Van Cleve

Page 69, © Elena Miras

Page 71, © Elena Miras

Page 75, © Don Singer

Page 77, © Elena Miras

Page 79, © Elena Miras

Page 80, © Elena Miras

Page 87, © Don Singer

Page 89, Photograph by Scott Frier; courtesy of
the U.S. Fish and Wildlife Service

Page 90, © Christie Van Cleve

Page 96, Photograph by Chad Olson; courtesy
of the National Park Service

Page 99, Photograph by Lisa Osborn; courtesy
of the author

Page 103, © Don Singer

Page 107, Courtesy of Barnes Bullets, Inc.

Page 110, © Glenn Oakley

Page 112, Photograph by Kris Lightner; courtesy
of the author

Page 117, Courtesy of the U.S. Fish and
Wildlife Service, Hopper Mountain NWRC

Page 119, © Elena Miras

Page 121, © Christie Van Cleve

Page 125, Photograph by Chad Olson; courtesy
of the National Park Service

Page 129, Courtesy of the U.S. Fish and
Wildlife Service, Hopper Mountain
NWRC

Page 135, © Elena Miras

Page 142, Photograph by Chad Olson; courtesy
of the National Park Service

Page 143, © Christie Van Cleve

Page 149, Courtesy of the author

Page 150, Photograph by Mark Lellouch;
courtesy of the National Park Service

continued next page

Sophie Osborn served as the Field Manager for the Peregrine Fund's California Condor Restoration Project in Arizona for three and one half years. Prior to working with condors, she received her Master's degree in Organismal Biology and Ecology at the University of Montana, where she studied American dippers, North America's only aquatic songbird. She has worked with more than a dozen bird species both nationally and internationally, and contributed to efforts to reintroduce peregrine falcons in the continental United States and Hawaiian crows in Hawaii. She has studied and helped conserve parrots in Guatemala, eagles in the cloud forest of Peru, and ducks in Argentina. She has authored numerous peer-reviewed articles on birds published in scientific journals. Osborn currently lives in Laramie, Wyoming, with her husband Chad and their two border collies.